A Marketer's Guide to Digital Advertising

A Marketer's Guide to Digital Advertising

Transparency, Metrics and Money

Shailin Dhar and Scott Thomson

KoganPage

First published in Great Britain and the United States in 2023 by Kogan Page Limited

2nd Floor, 45 Gee Street	8 W 38th Street, Suite 902	4737/23 Ansari Road
London	New York, NY 10018	Daryaganj
EC1V 3RS	USA	New Delhi 110002
United Kingdom		India

www.koganpage.com

Kogan Page books are printed on paper from sustainable forests.

ISBNs

Hardback   978 1 3986 0969 3
Paperback 978 1 3986 0966 2
Ebook   978 1 3986 0967 9

British Library Cataloguing-in-Publication Data

A CIP record for this book is available from the British Library.

Library of Congress Control Number
2023935275

Typeset by Integra Software Services, Pondicherry
Print production managed by Jellyfish
Printed and bound by CPI Group (UK) Ltd, Croydon, CR0 4YY

CONTENTS

ACKNOWLEDGMENTS

Our sincere and deepest gratitude to Cam, Stella, Stef, Marianna, Rob and Manuel, who have lived "transparency, metrics and money" in practice at MMI over the last year. You are all the most kind, dedicated, and thoughtful champions we've ever had the privilege of working with. But especially to Shikha and Sanjay, Janice and Joseph, our educators and moderators. Our "Maws and Das." Thanks for keeping us well-fed but also sending us out into the world with a hunger for more.

Introduction

Things change. Sometimes with a speed that's snail-like and almost imperceptible. At others with a velocity and scale that is nothing short of seismic. Like volcanic eruptions driven by hidden, slow-moving, tectonic shifts. And marketing is no different.

If you haven't witnessed a presentation in the last decade that has started with statements like "the pace of change is changing" or "digital is revolutionizing the industry" then you clearly haven't lived. Nor have you mingled at enough industry events if you haven't been exposed to phrases like "mass marketing is back" or "what's old is new again."

Changes are clearly afoot in marketing practice, and in often confusing and conflicting directions. And if you like sure bets, with clear guidelines that produce replicable advertising "wins," the digital age seems to offer conflicting assurance.

Advertisers who once had the relative luxury of a set of limited and finite choices now face a litany of options. Those who once could rely on internal company protocols that formulaically provided budget-setting guidelines, or effectiveness norms by media channel, now have no such playbooks to lean on.

Spending an advertising budget has always been risky. Whilst there is a perennial element of gambling involved, it has also always been an industry full of "informed choices." Choices that are sometimes, but not always, founded on great strategic insight and innovative creative executions. And framed, where possible, by as much granular feedback as deemed appropriate, or as technology and measurement approaches will allow.

And if the digital age has promised anything, it has promised that "granularity of feedback." Which it has delivered in spades, but not always of the type needed, nor wanted. As an industry, and particularly when it comes to data, we are not good at parsing what we *want* versus what we *need*.

And it could easily be argued that the ongoing explosion of data feeds and feedback loops hasn't helped, and that it has never been harder to operate as a marketing and advertising practitioner than it is now.

Choice and change in adland

On the one hand, there are more ways to reach consumers than there ever have been. Even the most complex TV advertising markets of the past 20 years only had up to 3,000 TV channels (e.g. in China). The modern digital buyer has, by contrast, and on paper at least, millions of options at their fingertips.

There are well over 1 billion available websites at the last count (Siteefy, 2022). And the ones that can be considered "active" (whilst less than 20 percent of that total) offer a hidden promise of incremental reach or frequency. More options might seem good, but this does somewhat represent a "curse of infinite choice."

For us humans, more choice tends to make us feel worse (Schwartz, 2004). The pain of losing out is often twice as much as the pain of a perceived win. And this is not akin to everyday regrets after making a selection amongst two or three options. What kind of buyer's remorse could we feel if there were a million other choices we *could have* made?

Plus, we just don't have the physical capacity for that kind of assessment. We are not made in a way that enables us to filter through countless options, assess them logically, and choose one. We are a bit fuzzier than that. We like rules of thumb. Basically, we don't "compute." Machines are good at that kind of thing though, and that's why the ad industry invented "programmatic" media buying.

Programmatic is simply the buying of digital advertising space through automated bidding techniques. Like an auction on steroids. It is made possible through the use of data and "machine learning" techniques to determine what ads to buy and how much to pay or bid for them. Ostensibly the use of software to buy digital media.

Or more specifically, it assesses and buys appropriate advertising opportunities *as they appear*. Because what is being "assessed" is not simply a website but the sudden and ephemeral appearance of a human on the web. And whether that human at that time in that place is what a specific advertiser wants.

This challenge of filtering through millions of options in a nanosecond was one that programmatic media buying technology has of course happily set itself up to solve.

For a price. And often a price that is not always apparent—because not all the players involved operate transparently, nor are they fully measurable. Which is akin to your new friendly automated buying machine saying, "I am not going to reveal how I have done what you have asked, just appreciate and bask in the glory of what I have just done for you."

No half measures

When you are spending millions, it's only fair that you demand measurement and some degree of transparency. How else can budgets be justified? Well, in many ways, just not all of them are based on rigorous science. Advertisers have a bit of a patchy history with such things. Not all of them are enamored with measurement as a practice. For some, rarely has a good measure got in the way of a great idea. And anyway, sometimes full and complete measurement simply wasn't possible. Certainly not in those good old analog days of "old media."

Digital promised to change that, but the promise of full unfettered measurement at scale has most definitely been unevenly fulfilled. Just because it is "digital" doesn't make it measurable. Feedback loops are often blocked, or faked. Transparencies trashed or neglected. As a result, there is an ongoing transparency crisis that one industry association refers to as "mind-numbingly" complex (ANA, 2021–22). And it's an opacity crisis mostly of the industry's own making. But also one that has been born of several other, oft-conflicting, forces. Combined, they make up a veritable "four horsemen" of a potential advertising apocalypse:

1 A fragmented media and consumer landscape with infinite complexities.
2 Potent but asymmetrically powerful tech platform partners.
3 Opaque supply chains and agency partner trading practices.
4 Regulatory and privacy mandates from authorities playing catch-up, but increasingly calling "foul."

A palpable "earth, water, wind and fire" of change that must be dealt with in the day job of an average campaign manager and his or her CMO.

How do we maximize engagement and minimize privacy infringement? How do we maximize reach across disparate fragmented spends? How do we count what counts and know if it really counted? How can we police Google and Facebook? Should we, can we?

These questions represent a set of issues that demand new skillsets and literacies that modern advertising job specifications should, but often do not, consider as prerequisites.

There is now an expectation for CMOs, and their teams, to be skilled in an array of topics. From having a grasp of the legal intricacies of privacy legislation, to having at least a surface understanding of web technology. From tackling the role and leverage of powerful tech platforms to maintaining relations with trusted buying partners who engage in a digital trading system that is byzantine at best, and fraudulent at worst.

Like most revolutions, this digital one has come with its own cast of heroes and villains. Good guys and bad guys, white hats and black hats. But with the villains not always instantly recognizable, nor revealed. The advertising industry now is awash with purveyors of the shiniest new technology. It is awash with middleware companies that have made fortunes and continue to do so.

It's also an industry full of doomsayers that cry it's all broken, full of snake oil salesmen and charlatans, and that the old way of doing things shouldn't be forgotten at the expense of a VC-backed tech start-up with references to "machine learning" in their portfolio of intellectual property.

Who to believe if you are an advertiser? It's a changing and challenging landscape for many. Full of friends and frenemies, tricks and traps, that line the path between you and your goals. If you are confused, you shouldn't be shy in admitting it.

Me, myself and ROI

Making a lasting impact, and effecting change itself, remain the ultimate demands for any advertising effort.

We are all in the behavior change business, be that driving short-term sales or building long-term consumer habits. Understanding what drives this, how to leverage it, maintain it, and measure it are the happy daily obsessions of good, productive marketeers.

Unless of course you, and your position itself, are a victim of an unwanted change.

Because marketers don't seem to hang around for too long, with circa 24 months being the current median tenure of a Chief Marketing Officer (Spencer Stuart, 2021/22), down from 30 months in the last two years alone.

Most of us have had relationships that lasted longer.

Which is particularly telling for the marketing and advertising industry, given that it involves those who are in the "relationship-building" business. It's an industry filled with romantic analogies of building "brand love," "loyalty," "suitability," "engagement," and "trust." Go figure.

There is an argument to be made that advertisers have never been so ill-prepared for the changes and choices that they currently face. And simultaneously so dependent on others. Because it has always been a collegiate industry. A bit like good filmmaking: dependent on internal teamwork and collaboration, supported by some specialized and outsourced skillsets.

Marketers today are increasingly at the mercy of those external partners and experts that they select and choose.

If it "takes a village to raise a child," it can sometimes seem that now it takes a midsized metropolitan population just to get a modern campaign up and running and connected to your own digital infrastructure. Data scientists, programmatic specialists, ad traffickers, JavaScript engineers, cloud infrastructure specialists, verification partners, auditors, and lawyers all get a look in. And that's just on a Monday.

This explosion in options and scale of choices, and the number and nature of characters involved, has coincided with an apparent decrease in the industry's ability to *effect any change*. Period.

ROIs have been decreasing (IPA, 2019) at a time when we were promised greater efficiencies and better outcomes born of a digital and data revolution. Granted, there have been counterclaims from the industry that these declines are only temporary and have simply coincided with a period of "flux" whilst the industry simply grapples with, and learns from, experimenting with shiny new toys (see e.g. Kite, 2022).

Either way, it's not great that the potency of advertising is under question when we have so many more tools and approaches to facilitate and deliver it. Remember, the digital marketing revolution is over 20 years old, and it could easily be claimed that *never has more choice been facilitated by so many for so long to impact so few*. At scale. And for a premium.

Gods in the machines

Adland is now clearly less about the chemical alchemy of a great creative execution, and more about the physics of AdTech, data, and digital traffic, with partnerships and unions formed at an altar of data-driven "personalization" and "refined targeting."

But it's also an industry that is experiencing a significant crisis. A crisis of faith and trust in the very partners relied upon, with clear power imbalances, privacy demands, fragmented contractual partnerships, as well as ongoing identity management and legal challenges.

If it's a mid-life crisis for your average marketeer, then it's one where ways of working and thinking that once were thought of as "good bets" are now being cast aside for a series of shiny new objects that promise precision and efficiency. Using technologies that are often mystical for legacy practitioners.

A badlands of modern marketing. Where established maps are meaningless, and partners may not have our interests at heart.

It is a vast and growing commercial landscape.

The total global advertising market is currently worth $766 billion, and it's projected that this number will exceed $1 trillion by 2025, with way more than half of that spent on digital outreach. Clearly a sector with a lot of growth and superficial health.

But it's controlled by only a few players, as illustrated in Figure 0.1. Around 75 cents of every digital ad dollar now go to three companies: Alphabet (Google), Meta (Facebook), and Amazon Ad Services.

Which of course has created a significant power imbalance, has threatened the very leverage that agency holding groups were built upon, and made advertisers themselves question what power and influence they have, if any, on the digital choices they face.

Advertisers and their agents remain hostage to announcements and updates from these powerful platform owners, driven by the emergence of an era of privacy concerns. These announcements rightly claim that they will protect the quality of consumer experiences and hold their privacies sacrosanct.

In many ways, though, privacy requirements have been weaponized.

They are used to gain competitive advantage over one another, whilst simultaneously virtue-signaling to their consumer base and those legislators waiting in the wings to break up their monopolies. The "closed web" players have been accused of using privacy mandates as a stick to beat each other

Figure 0.1 Global digital ad platform shares

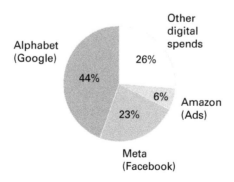

with. The "open web" players and anyone asking about data access are also being fended off with the same gambit.

Transparencies are sacrificed by some, and lack of transparencies justified by others. All this weighs together to make that precariously positioned CMO's job harder, largely because of a lack of that one critical tool in any good CMO's box of tricks. The one that was the overarching promise of the digital revolution in the first place—useful measurement.

An industry crying "foul"

Trade associations representing these advertisers are increasingly crying foul. The largest of these, the ANA (Association of National Advertisers) in the United States, in 2021 announced another investigation into an industry that is "subject to arbitrage, mark-ups, rebates, proprietary and opaque algorithms, data transparency issues, a myriad of dataset costs, and a plethora of charges that have not been fully exposed" (ANA, 2021–22).

This follows on from a previous FBI probe into the everyday habits of several industry players (McCarthy, 2018), with showcase trials and convictions of several fraudsters, and multiple ongoing anti-competitive enquiries being run by a series of national governments across the globe.

The perceived scale of fraudulent activity surrounding digital advertising varies. What everyone does agree on is that its financial impact runs into the tens of billions ("$6.5B–$19B"), with several third-party consultants putting that figure much higher ("$34B" to "increase to $87B") (Perrin, 2019; TrafficGuard and Juniper, 2020)

The World Federation of Advertisers has predicted that, by 2025, ad fraud might become second only to the drug trade for organized crime (WFA, 2016).

That's always worth repeating. The global trade association for the advertising industry, representing over 80 percent of global advertisers, and tasked with setting global industry standards, predicts that the second biggest potential source of money for global organized crime will be the digital advertising ecosystem.

With the one fundamental caveat being that it's not that "organized." It's more "organic" than you think. As we will point out later, the largest threat to ad budgets does not come from shady and connected characters in some faraway land, but from everyday industry practices and a patchwork-like infrastructure that is open to being gamed—by *anyone*.

This is an industry that has porous walls. And one which is easily gamed, with fraudulent activity being easy to attempt, with few barriers and little or low risk. Convictions and prosecutions remain rare and are limited to only a few high-profile cases and countries (DOJ, 2021).

So as a modern marketer running digital advertising, you may face an unknown landscape, with millions of choices, full of technologies you may only be casually familiar with, peppered with malicious players, with partners you may be losing trust in, and working a system that may be treating your money like a Japanese Pachinko machine.

Apart from that, everything is fine, the industry is in rude health, and fortunes are being made.

Apocalypse delayed

How can this system maintain itself, and not be corrected, you may ask?

Will the AdTech bubble burst? And why hasn't this potential "Ad Apocalypse" happened yet? The reasons are multiple as we will later discover.

Many would contend that change in the industry has always been associated with periods of inefficiency. Remember, this is an industry that for 100 years has happily lived with the John Wanamaker/Lord Leverhulme mantra that "half of my advertising budget is wasted, I just don't know which half." Even though the industry, comically, can't even seem to agree which one of these two cats to attribute this quote to.

Some would even say that this "glass half full" statement is a bit optimistic at times. Ours has never been an industry with a foundation in precision or "uber efficiency". It has traditionally been more of a craft skill than a science.

Bad practice is also nothing new. Kickbacks, hidden rebates, bribes, breaches, and the falsification of data were all present before digital ad fraud was born.

What is now unique is *the sheer automated and industrial scale of such activity*.

Machines don't have morals. And all their questionable activity happens out of sight. Which helps sustain a sense of normality. Bad things only happen if we see them, right?

While we can all breathe a pre-emptive sigh of relief at the delaying of the ad-apocalypse, others would say this reckoning is still nigh.

These doomsayers do tend to have a vested interest in that kind of messaging. And they tend to be independent ad fraud researchers, and they have been part of the advertising industry chattersphere for several years.

We know many of them personally. We even consider some of them friends.

They often act as inadvertent fire-starters, but that's not always their fault. As any journalist worth their salt would testify, the sort of stuff they peddle is gold, and there has always been a home for apocalyptic narratives, from the Bible all the way through to Chicken Little.

They are, though, smart enough not to provide fixed predictions with hard dates. Offering fixed dates and hard verifiable figures is a bad strategy if you are a doomsayer.

Hence the numerous "it's all fraudulent!" headlines, the large numbers, and the bundled and often convenient definitions that add potency to a narrative that can be counterproductive—sometimes at the expense of the thing that we know many of these characters hold dear, namely being a useful catalyst for industry change.

The numbers quoted are vast and varied. And it's easy to see why. Those who are familiar with the mechanics of the trade will understand that most quoted ad fraud figures don't relate to invalid traffic (IVT) in and of itself—but can be comprised of a combination of IVT rates, plus lack of viewability, false reporting, fake installs, misattribution, and even retained and undeclared trading monies.

Talking up their market is one thing, but the doomsayers are also sometimes guilty of an inadvertent conflation of "sub-optimal ad operations" (of which all of the above things are evidence), and "lack of digital advertising effectiveness" (which those things contribute to but aren't the sole cause of). Sometimes ads just suck.

We must be able to parse "doing the right thing" in terms of effectiveness, from "doing things well" in terms of efficiency. It helps us navigate and provides guidelines on what to do next.

A new map

Independent doomsayer researchers are often marginal voices in the industry. Treated like skeptics and cynics on the sidelines. Industry party poopers. Or as one commentator put it, "dogs that bark whilst the gypsy caravan moves on." They are not the industry's sole source of salvation, but we do need them. They are sometimes very right.

Some analysts are right to point to a systematic malaise in the industry in terms of sub-optimal buying behaviors, the associated use of available datasets and platforms (AANA 2021), and indeed the increasing lack of effectiveness in digital advertising investment, period.

And of course, all these things must be addressed in the right order—address sub-optimal behaviors and measurement techniques in the digital ecosystem, and only then can anyone get to grips with attribution.

Before we approach attribution, we must make sure that data is kosher and that counts are good.

When it comes to basic counts though, there are often multiple conflicting versions of a truth. As is often the case in the digital measurement and verification space, for example, where there are multiple players who all claim to measure fraud but can never agree on the numbers.

It's a Rashomon-like industry where there are multiple conflicting versions of events tending to only preserve each teller's self-interest. There are some who claim to have better mousetraps than others to approach a more holistic and valid estimate of ad fraud. They tend to be "more right" than the others.

Being right, though, is not enough, nor always useful. Power and influence are needed for that. Plus, the data they produce must have *some* actionable use.

A measure of ad fraud is meaningless if it can't *be acted upon*. And advertisers and their agencies must find utility in the numbers that verification companies provide. Otherwise, the numbers that a whole side of the industry actively produce are relegated to being nothing more than political placebos. Something to point at when asked, "do we have transparency?"

A useful and transparent map of your digital spending will only appear if (i) you find verification measurements that are *right plus useful*, and (ii) the scale of those measures reaches as far as is allowed in the Open Web.

As an industry we have not been very successful at self-policing. Regulatory authorities are waiting in the wings to help us get our act together and are increasingly showing signs of having lost patience. Many would argue though that multiple government attempts to regulate the industry have been misguided at best, and toothless at worst.

More think that it is advertisers themselves that must lean in more, and we tend to agree. Making themselves more digitally literate, and less dependent on third parties. Developing their internal capabilities where it is wise and not just fashionable. And pooling their resources and influence via their trade associations.

At least now there is a growing sense that it is *digital signals themselves* that are often the key tools when the system is being gamed. *Machines tricking other machines* with bid requests and faked code strings.

Being right and useful with your metrics is the best way to navigate those "horsemen" of the Ad Apocalypse. Putting available datasets and partners to work in a way that is privacy-friendly can be daunting, but marketers must do so themselves to unpack opaque supply chains and trading practices to navigate that messy middle.

In this book, that's what we will show you how to do.

We will do so from a perspective born of practice, given that, between us, we have close to 50 years of experience in the industry across multiple markets, as advertising clients, agency practitioners, auditors, consultants, and tech suppliers. We know what marketers want, the nature of agency-holding companies, what technology can and cannot currently do, and even how to game the system if you ask us nicely.

We will also do so in a manner that keeps jargon to a minimum. It's a complicated ecosystem, and the terminology doesn't help.

And that's the first place we want to start. To give you a grounding in the foundational elements of the web, to make sure we can help you bridge practical knowledge gaps. Without that context, it can get a bit lost.

Language and intangibles

Language itself helps bridge knowledge gaps.

But it is also a trap. It can often conceal as much as it reveals; a soothing placebo for superficial understanding. A convenient heuristic. A mask.

It is often said that experts in digital advertising have created their own obscure language to describe the ecosystem to their paying clients. Advertisers are often blinded by these complexities, peddled by their closest trusted partners. "What exactly do you mean by the 'bid-stream'?" they ask. "What the heck is 'pre-bid,' in simple terms?" "Or 'post-bid,' for that matter."

It can equally be said that wider society has adopted some terms that can be counterproductive when trying to describe the engineering infrastructure of the internet. The very history of language surrounding the internet is peppered with strange but soothing metaphors.

"Walled gardens" itself is a perennial, used to elicit some kind of pleasant, inaccessible, benign, moneyed, privileged-but-safe curated space somewhere over there... "in the Cloud," which itself might soon be as dated as "cyberspace."

The upside of this language trap is that it changes and cycles over time, making it possible to move in better directions in the future. A vague sense of time and change, however, will be of no solace to those currently trying to navigate a path for their organization whilst they listen to the stream of information supplied by their agencies and partners.

The other great asset of tech land, information and data itself, can also be a bit formless, like an intangible asset that we often do our best to describe with other handy metaphors. Sometimes they were created by people who were very excited about the internet and were trying to explain it to people who didn't understand it at all. Or venture capitalists. Or government officials re-hashing older phrases in cringe-inducing interrogations of the CEOs of "big tech" at congressional hearings.

The language or vocabulary used in any context is dependent on the person using it and their political intent.

"The metaphor of the Internet as the information superhighway was chosen deliberately to demonstrate the utility and everyday nature of the Internet over the utopian vision of cyberspace that had informed its early development," wrote professors Cornelius Puschmann and Jean Burgess. When "cyberspace" was used, it was used to describe a place that governments must bring under control, whilst the "information highway" is invoked by activists trying to keep it free. What can start as a metaphor for regulation and markets, can end up as a symbol of freedom (Puschmann and Burgess, 2014).

Empires have been built on such language. Facebook itself relies on the notion of friendship as a metaphor for connectivity. A very utopian notion of connectivity. A somewhat California-esque dream of a connected but decentralized world that simultaneously offers security.

Which is of course only being repeated as they lurch towards, and invest billions in, the metaverse. But when pushed by legislators in a US Congressional hearing to describe in plain terms what they do, Mark Zuckerberg politely said, "Senator, we sell ads."

All of this belies a tangible, underlying physical truth of the internet. It masks us from the physical reality of data centers and underwater cables. Once we grasp that, it's easier to see how it can be gamed.

Thanks to Amazon, which launched its Elastic Compute Cloud service in 2006, the term "the Cloud" is now used to describe any remote data storage and computing.

It's weightless and intentionally vague: your data is up there somewhere, in a better place, where you can forget about it. It's in sharp contrast to the industrial reality of millions of remote servers, tucked sometimes underground in data centers that are gigantic, loud, and require tremendous amounts of energy.

We may imagine the digital cloud as placeless, mute, ethereal, and unmediated. Yet the reality of the cloud is embodied in thousands of these massive data centers.

In his book *A Prehistory of the Cloud*, Tung-Hui Hu examined this gap between the real and the virtual in our understanding of it (Hu, 2015). Behind that cloud-shaped icon on our screens is a whole universe of technologies all working to keep us from noticing their existence.

At the time of writing, there are over 7 million such data centers spread across the planet, any one of which can use as much electricity as a midsized town. They are also, notably, the biggest contributor of carbon emissions in global IT.

Advertising has fully mechanized itself off the back of them. And like many industries before, it is now having its "moment" of disruptive change— for good or bad.

This enables these faceless servers to trade and deliver advertising content at scale. Making billions of daily trades. Storing zettabytes of data, some of it benign, some of it very personal.

But how secure is it in reality? Can the trading of advertising opportunities be gamed? And the delivery of ad content spoofed? Can those server-initiated requests be made to appear of human origin? And can they trick both human governance and indeed other machines themselves?

This last question is a pivotal one for the veracity of the digital ecosystem. As we will point out later, it is this very ability for machine-on-machine trickery that sits at the epicenter of many of the inefficiencies in the advertising ecosystem. And remember, "inefficiencies" tends to be code for *your money being lost in the ether.*

Wo/man and machine

The so-called "Turing Test" allows all of us to access and estimate the "humanness" of a machine. The extent to which it passes as familiar or seems a bit "uncanny." A lot has been written about this, and much of entertainment culture has drawn upon the narrative of the happy/sad android who just wants to be treated with human dignity. It's a narrative that goes all the way back to Pinocchio.

But there is little public discussion or energy devoted to whether computers can reliably know when they themselves are interacting with another computer or a human. Or specifically, machine-on-machine trickery.

A machine's ability to appear human to humans has been well established. That box was ticked a long time ago with the advent of MIT's ELIZA in the mid-'60s (Weizenbaum, 1976). An early natural language processing tool, and the granny of all chatbots, ELIZA could engage in simple discourse, but she was still fundamentally incapable of true understanding.

ELIZA only delivered an illusion of understanding. But her creators were amazed at the number of people who attributed human-like feelings to her outpourings, and many early users were convinced of her intelligence and understanding, despite her creator's insistence to the contrary.

More recently, a Google employee in 2022 claimed that a chatbot he was working on was definitively showing evidence of becoming "sentient" (Luscombe, 2022). But a "HAL"-like chatbot friend may or may not be with us just yet, and it does remain an open question just how successfully any machine can fully replicate human qualities in a digital context.

Whilst ELIZA and many modern-day chatbots still fail in this regard, they still have their utility; interacting with ELIZA proved to be very therapeutic for many. The lesson is that it doesn't take that much to trigger our innate desire to attribute belief in something being human. We want to humanize things. And the threshold required for a machine to appear human to a human user is, as a result, quite a low bar.

It does beg the question: does this also hold true for "machine to machine" trickery? How successful are machines at appearing human to other machines?

A large chunk of the industry's AdTech stacks are focused on helping determine "how human-like" any online activity appears. The industry is obsessed with tracking things like mouse movements to help determine whether a given behavior seems kosher. The measurement side of the industry has built a collective obsession with "what does human activity look like online?" As a result, a plethora of ad verification suppliers have built up an arsenal of tools that are focused on tracking and modeling behaviors.

Unfortunately, many of these approaches are like trying to spot counterfeit currency notes by looking at a photocopy. Human activity can be emulated. Mouse movements can be spoofed. Behavioral tracking tricked. Accelerometer signals simulated. Gyroscope sensor data falsified.

Verification methods based on such techniques can be got around, utilizing digital interpretations of human actions. Rather than validating human operability, some techniques have proven detrimental to the sanctity of accurate measurement. Just because these techniques are prevalent doesn't make them right.

But that's only part of the trickery involved, and some would say the hardest part. Emulating human behavior at a device level is one thing, but there is an easier route to stealing an ad budget. And that involves spoofing the signals in the trading of ad opportunities itself. Machines tricking machines at the most basic level.

Beneath the surface, the ad industry remains a system that is open to manipulation by this specific type of trickery. It can be easily "gamed" with a casual line of code. This is significant because it can be done *at scale and at speed*.

It is perfect for machines to trick other machines in the "bid stream."

"What the heck is the 'bid stream'?" I hear you ask, echoing our befuddled CMO. Put simply, it refers to the transactional part of the programmatic market system, as opposed to the actual ad delivery part of the system. Which is another piece of foundational knowledge that we want to make sure you have before we go any further.

Trading versus delivery systems

Figure 0.2 shows a simple illustration of how machines book digital media, and how ad content is delivered (using connected TV (CTV) campaigns as an example).

Figure 0.2 Trading versus delivery systems in digital buying for connected television

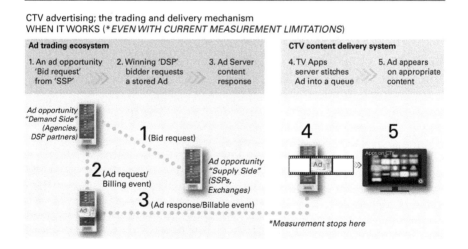

There is a trading system, and a delivery system, in the very same way that there is the act of ordering a pizza, and that pizza's delivery. The two are usually connected but *aren't always*. Orders can exist without deliveries.

This is significant because it helps with understanding not only the role of different machines at different times, but also the points at which any ad system is vulnerable to being tricked.

The overall ecosystem that supports the global advertising industry is one that is extremely susceptible to different types of malicious attacks at different places using an array of techniques. We will explore some of these techniques and their significance in other chapters, and show research that outlines how the CTV space in particular is now being gamed in this manner.

But keeping a broad distinction between this trading vs. delivery system as part of your mental map is important. Regardless of whether an end user is using a laptop, smartphone, or increasingly a smart TV, this distinction is key to putting in place strategies that will keep your money safe and mitigate the risk of paying to advertise to "bad bots."

An ad system built with porous walls

Circa 50 percent of internet traffic as we currently know it is driven by bots that are invisible to the human eye. Pinging each other via a global infrastructure of underground data centers and subterranean cables, not all of them malicious nor overly sophisticated but an oft-essential by-product of the way we increasingly live.

This is a virtual non-human web, funded by, and focused on, one thing: advertising dollars.

When bots are bad, they are not necessarily sophisticated. Ones that exist on your device mimicking your behavior can be, but the ones that sit in the trading part of the ad ecosystem only have to follow the rule sets of other bots for not attracting unwanted attention. And therein lies the rub.

As we will outline, the vast majority of simple and scalable bots that are designed to siphon ad dollars can be found in the very data centers that the ad industry funds.

They hide in the web's infrastructure. Not in the backrooms of some malicious crime syndicate-sponsored hacker sitting in an exotic foreign locale, but down the road, in the neighborhood, and inside part of the infrastructure that industry has helped build. This is not the old cybersecurity world of "infected local machines" or "bot networks." This is a remote world, with much simpler code, that sits in apparently benign data centers casually skimming ad budgets based on machine-on-machine trickery.

Who is at fault and who is to blame? Are the public-facing giant technology platforms an easily recognizable target? Or is there something else at play that undermines the integrity of adland?

The simple answer is "everyone, yes, and many things." Which we will go into over the course of the next few chapters. Before we get there, though, it's important to grasp from the outset that the digital advertising system is a mash-up of many technologies.

And each element of it is largely task-dependent. For example, Google's DV360 may help you book media with ease, sourcing traffic from exchanges such as OpenX or Appnexus, AWS may help you ingest subsequent measurement bid stream data, processes and storing it at scale, and your data science team might draw upon SQL or Python skillsets to make the messy magical.

And connections must be set up, and adaptations made dependent on specific set-ups. Measurement tags that work on one platform may not work on others. If tags are erroneous, connections are lost, and data disappears.

Things often break, and the industry is awash with daily meetings between account managers and AdTech engineers from publishers, agencies and measurement firms poring over the minutiae of tags and set-ups. It's a constant battle just to make sure that campaigns run, measurement is in place, and the data and money are flowing.

Running digital campaigns, setting them up and maintaining them can be a messy and frustrating pastime. And the industry doesn't always attract the requisite engineering skills required to solve some of the daily campaign and measurement set-up challenges. It's often speculated that engineers are not attracted to AdTech because they may end up with a set of banal and horrible tasks to fulfill. But it's also an industry full of complicated tasks and nutty problems to solve.

And there are obviously engineering skillsets on the "dark side" of that exploitation line, which, ironically, often use tools from the very companies that help the kosher side.

As our own research has demonstrated, browser bots designed to siphon ad money from the industry can use automation tools that are *developed and maintained by Google and Microsoft*, and can be deployed at enormous scale using cloud computing technologies *provided by Amazon (AWS), Google (GCP), and Microsoft (Azure)* (MMI, 2020).

These developer tools are an essential part of the arsenal of good engineers. For example, they help developers streamline web testing, monitor websites, or aggregate content. They help the engineering world go round by automating repetitive tasks. But they are regularly hijacked by engineers with other things in mind. Good tools are being used for malicious purposes they weren't designed for.

All of which makes the digital advertising ecosystem wide open for exploitation. From the cracks between the pipes, or the tools the industry uses.

It's a moveable feast of problems for people working at the coal face of the industry. An industry made up of a patchwork quilt of different technologies, that was never designed to be "watertight." That's because it was never *designed* as a system in its entirety. If we were collectively starting from scratch, it wouldn't be built this way, but it is.

Investing time and money in the digital advertising ecosystem demands certain daily habits that you and your partners must foster if you are to avoid common pitfalls.

Ultimately, this is a story about people, and their relationship with technology. More specifically, it's about decision makers in advertising, their agents, and their relationship with technology. As in, they don't always have one, not in a sense that would be recognized by a web engineer, anyway.

It could be argued that advertisers and their proxies don't need to know how the internet works. Just that it does, for their purposes.

As one CMO recently said to us, "I don't have time to determine whether 30 percent of my digital ad budget globally has been stolen, I am the damn CMO." They sometimes just want most of the rest of what they do to demonstrably shine.

But if any knowledge gap interferes with that efficacy, or any structural inefficiency exists, then the onus is on them to bridge that gap—or at least on someone in their orbit, a trusted source and preferably a polite one.

Sometimes that big dramatic change happens, and sometimes it doesn't. And sometimes that shiny new digital technology is brilliant, and sometimes it isn't.

If you are a manager of any sort of modern marketing, you are faced with choices. You must choose how to respond to potential catalysts for change, when to opportunistically take advantage of them, and when to ignore them.

This remains the beating heart of good marketing management, with measurement increasingly at its epicenter. But it's a beating heart that finds itself in a very new digitally driven context, with a consumer base less reliant on real-life connections, in a world of delivery apps and socio-political online media bubbles. Of disinformation and misinformation. With the largely ad-funded "walled gardened" giants of social media and e-commerce being potent daily touchstones for many.

We are all "digital natives" now. And as practitioners in the evolving trades of marketing and advertising, we all need to update our maps and form new habits.

That is what we will help you do.

References

AANA (2021) Are We There Yet? programmatic practice study 2021, https://aana.com.au/2021/02/23/are-we-there-yet/ (archived at https://perma.cc/95QY-K4XT)

ANA (2021–22) Association of National Advertisers, ongoing Programmatic Transparency Study, https://www.ana.net/content/show/id/pr-2021-programmatic-rfp (archived at https://perma.cc/3NPJ-XHSS)

DOJ (2021) Russian Cybercriminal Sentenced to 10 Years in Prison for Digital Advertising Fraud Scheme, https://www.justice.gov/usao-edny/pr/russian-cybercriminal-sentenced-10-years-prison-digital-advertising-fraud-scheme (archived at https://perma.cc/7CLZ-ZNEF)

Hu, T-H (2015) *A Prehistory of the Cloud*, MIT Press

IPA (2019) Effectiveness Database, https://ipa.co.uk/awards-events/effectiveness-awardsv1/ease (archived at https://perma.cc/ZKU5-ESKL)

Kite, G (2022) We've been worrying about a crisis in effectiveness, new data shows it's over, *Magic Numbers*, https://magicnumbers.co.uk/articles/weve-been-worrying-about-a-crisis-in-effectiveness-new-data-shows-its-over/ (archived at https://perma.cc/BC4M-M4BP)

Luscombe, R (2022) Google engineer put on leave after saying AI chatbot has become sentient, *Guardian*, https://www.theguardian.com/technology/2022/jun/12/google-engineer-ai-bot-sentient-blake-lemoine (archived at https://perma.cc/8QRQ-DS6U)

McCarthy, J (2018) ANA informs defrauded advertisers how to aid FBI media buying investigation, *The Drum*, https://www.thedrum.com/news/2018/10/10/ana-informs-defrauded-advertisers-how-aid-fbi-media-buying-investigation (archived at https://perma.cc/UQ6G-7UYY)

MMI (2020) In Plain Sight: How developer tools enable invalid traffic, https://www.methodmi.com/reports/in-plain-sight (archived at https://perma.cc/G7H2-ECCP)

Perrin, N (2019) Digital Ad Fraud 2019, *Insider Intelligence*, https://www.insiderintelligence.com/content/digital-ad-fraud-2019 (archived at https://perma.cc/K28Y-R766)

Puschmann, C and Burgess, J (2014) Big data, big questions: Metaphors of big data *International Journal of Communications*, 8, https://ijoc.org/index.php/ijoc/article/view/2169 (archived at https://perma.cc/6YBK-FZV3)

Schwartz, B (2004) *The Paradox of Choice*, Ecco

Siteefy (2022) How many websites are there in the world? https://siteefy.com/how-many-websites-are-there/ (archived at https://perma.cc/R7D2-C7PP)

Spencer Stuart (2021/22) CMO Tenure Study, https://www.spencerstuart.com/research-and-insight/cmo-tenure-study-progress-for-women-less-for-racial-diversity (archived at https://perma.cc/BHG5-PPG4); https://www.spencerstuart.com/research-and-insight/cmo-tenure-study-women-outnumber-men-for-first-time-in-cmo-role (archived at https://perma.cc/5TA2-SEKT)

TrafficGuard and Juniper (2020) Ad fraud at '$34B' and will 'increase to $87B' within two years, https://www.trafficguard.ai/resources/digital-ad-fraud-in-north-america-infographic (archived at https://perma.cc/7VZJ-AWEP)

US Congressional hearings (2018) Mark Zuckerberg explaining the internet at 2018 Congressional Hearings

Weizenbaum, J (1976) *Computer Power and Human Reason*, WH Freeman & Co

WFA (2016) Ad Fraud Report, https://wfanet.org/knowledge/item/2016/06/06/WFA-issues-first-advice-for-combatting-ad-fraud (archived at https://perma.cc/TRP5-QYPF)

Meaningful measurement 01

Brands and their advertising agencies continue to pour ad dollars into parts of their media mix that are sometimes known, and sometimes not known, to be opaque and unaccountable.

As outlined in the introduction, this coincides with conflicting evidence on whether advertising effectiveness is in decline, with the only signal of success sometimes being from the platform operators themselves.

As good marketers you will always want to find partners that help change this dynamic—or at least work with those that can simultaneously demystify and improve how much bang you are getting for your buck.

There is one question that we always like to ask advertisers when we first start working with them, and it is this: "*If you could choose one thing, would you want to (i) do the right thing in the first instance or (ii) do what you are doing very very well?*"

It is, of course, a bit of a Sophie's Choice of a question. It's like asking whether you would like effectiveness or efficiency. You ideally would want to attain both. But in more cases than not, we get a singular answer, and it gives us a sense of the kind of advertiser we are working with.

Some people are convinced that what they are currently doing is correct, and the only thing they need is a bit of efficiency: "Identify waste, eliminate it, optimize our spends, help us work towards greater effectiveness." Others are more concerned about making sure they have both the right kind of messaging and media mix (the selection of media formats and channels identified as appropriate for gaining the attention of potential customers). They assess all their partners and pose more fundamental and unified sets of questions.

Sometimes, but rarely, we also come across a third type: those who are less concerned with efficiencies but for a different reason. They have a conviction that any waste will be mitigated by the above-average impact of what can be done by "doing the right thing" anyways. They have faith that the potency of their approach far outweighs the losses associated with any inefficiencies of spend.

All these perspectives and approaches require very different types of measurement. Different feedback loops, different areas of focus.

Whilst some might skew towards "am I getting what I paid for?", others might be more focused on "is what I am doing working?" and helping to establish if what you are doing is "right" in the first place.

Measure what matters, where you can

There tend to be classic "buckets" of scores that an advertising practitioner looks for. Nothing exists in a vacuum. And most digital campaigns are part of a wider level of digital and non-digital spending. Table 1.1 gives an overview of the three typical types of measurement that any digital ad practitioner will naturally have a sense of.

It is of course imperative that you tie your campaigns to specific desired campaign scores and eventual outcomes. And those outcomes can of course have varying degrees of immediate "performance-based" versus longer-haul "brand-based" goals.

It's also rife with danger. "What gets measured gets managed" is the oft-quoted platitude. But this can be misleading. Put simply, it does assume that what you are measuring is worthy of management in the first place. The full mantra goes as follows:

"What gets measured gets managed—even when it's pointless to measure and manage it, and even if it harms the purpose of the organization to do so."

Table 1.1   Fundamental digital measurement requirements

1. **Transactional/ currency measures**	Audience measurement/counts
	Audience segments/IDs
	Audience verification
2. **Impact measures**	Campaign metrics
	Brand health measures
	Sales impacts

(continued)

Table 1.1 (Continued)

3. **Attributional metrics and analytics that connect 1&2**	Probabilistic outcome analytics that demand statistical inference
	Deterministic outcome measures that require little or no analytics

Which is better because it at least makes you start thinking about whether your chosen KPIs are worthy in the first place, and what they are doing for the wider health of your company.

"Just because it can be measured doesn't mean you should" is another phrase that should be on a t-shirt.

If it ever came in memo form, then the industry has largely missed that one.

Readily available *campaign metrics* have come in more useless forms than anyone could have imagined. At least basic *campaign counts* like impressions serve as a basic form of currency. But the number of "likes" or "followers," even "page views" and "clicks" are often nothing more than vanity metrics.

Connecting such "intermediate" campaign metrics to valued outcomes has always been a noble ambition. And tying KPIs to your strategy.

Which is where, of course, good analysts come in.

But they in turn can only work with what you give them. Their job (particularly the ROI attribution part) has only become harder. If you get a gaggle of econometricians together and ask them nicely these days, they will tend to admit that building good models for useful and comprehensive advertising attribution is becoming near impossible.

If you give them bad data to work with, it doesn't matter how many mathematical somersaults they do, they will never be able to build viable models, nor give precise attributional analysis for what your campaign produced in terms of sales, and what parts worked well.

This is why the foundational metrics—particularly the most basic kind in terms of valid audience counts—matter so much. You can't build models on sand.

It's at this point that we spell out that they may not yet have a choice in the matter anyway. Either because the most basic data is unavailable or because there are no independent validators of the data that is made available.

Just because a form of media is digitally driven, doesn't make it inherently measurable. Assuming "it's digital therefore measurable" is also a danger. And independent measurement is not always a given.

The industry is currently in a situation where a massive percentage of total ad spend goes to forms of media whose principles of measurement are untouched by any form of independent evaluation or audit (see Figure 1.1).

It seems odd to think of a "measurement deficit" existing across an industry that is so data-rich. And even when there is a richness of measurement, it comes from disparate sources and is often conflicting.

In one sense efforts here can be very much focused on simply aligning with differing versions of the truth. One classic example of this, as we will go into some detail about in a moment, is how many "impressions" you got, which is largely dependent on who you ask (i.e. which company's database along the supply chain did you query) and what definition of "impression" they are using.

Of course, the measurement of ultimate outcomes has little to do with how many impressions, or clicks, or likes you achieved, and has everything to do with how much you impacted your business goals. Be that sales or orders or another KPI. The measurement challenge here is often one of

Figure 1.1   Industry measurement map

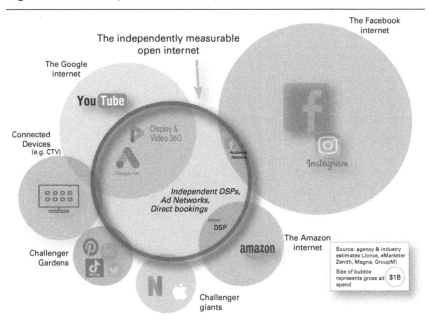

Agency and industry estimates from Jonce, eMarketer, Zenith, Magna, and GroupM

connecting intermediate digital campaign metrics with wider measures using some kind of holistic, and probabilistic, modeling. Just having the data doesn't lead to any outcomes-focused insight—and the reality check here relates to the difficulties associated with connecting disparate datasets from different sources.

Rarely, outside of the context of e-commerce, is there a deterministic direct link that is easily made from digital campaign exposure to sale.

Counting impressions

The thing about ad impressions is that it depends on when you are calculating them and who is doing the calculations.

Impressions are not static, unchangeable things. The number of impressions that are measured depends on who is measuring them, and the *point at which* they are being measured.

The official definition of an impression is something akin to the following—*an ad creative that is shown on an ad property that is fully loaded onto a web page and shown to an actual user.*

But there are different stages in the delivery of that ultimate goal, different points of an "impression's" journey. And resultant differences in terms of charging, based on a billable event which is based on when a particular part of the supply chain is "done" with handling the impression in question.

It's like a game of hot potato, with no guarantee of comparable counts.

If you are a web content publisher (be you a streaming channel, a website, or a mobile app) your systems (SSP, or supply-side partner) make an ad request (or a call flagging an opportunity for someone to bid on an available ad slot as a result of a visitor). This then goes through an exchange which then talks to the buy-side and their systems (or DSPs, demand-side platforms). Bids are made, at scale, in milliseconds. Winning bids then go through another wave of tech, primarily ad servers, which are focused on the delivery of actual ad content.

Everything before the actual ad server "counting" (when the actual ad content is delivered and rendered and a strictly defined impression made) is essentially incomplete transactions.

But this doesn't stop everyone involved referring to their own version of "impressions," be they **complete** or otherwise. Be they **valid** or not. Be they sourced from the trading or delivery part of the process.

Both you and your partners must be precise about measurement.

And the natural incentives to do so may not be in place. After all, the more traffic a media partner reports, the more valuable they seem, the more traffic a buyer generates, the more bang they seem to be getting for your buck.

But you have to ensure that everyone around you at least uses precision in the language they use when talking about traffic and impression counts. Do not, for example, let anyone casually use the phrase "impressions" without making sure you are clear about what they mean. It could cost you, especially if you are being billed by volume-based units like CPMs. There is typically, for example, around a 10 percent discrepancy between impression counts based on the trading part of the system ("auctions won") versus those at the delivery side ("ads served").

We have seen many clients who are unsure of the basis of their billing mechanics. At this most basic level. And it saves them money before any further measurement work or analysis commences.

Once you have established these basics, you can then go one step further and check the validity of the counts themselves. Are all these counts human or bots? Those interactions exposed to an ad have to be validated as actual humans.

Which in and of itself is critical in an ad environment where circa 50 percent of events are associated with bots (Imperva, 2021), many of which are necessary ones that help the internet work, and nasty ones that are out to get you.

Buying bought impressions

Impressions are bought.

Let's rephrase that. Of course, media buyers try to buy impressions. It's the trading currency *du jour* after all. But they might be buying impressions that have themselves been bought. And these sets of bought impressions can get past prevalent industry quality checks. And these bought impressions may be sourced from bots. Or as one industry observer succinctly puts it, with tongue firmly in cheek: "Media buyers may buy impressions that are bought from bots that bypass the best bot detection."

The economic pressures for some publishers tempt them to go to bought sources of traffic and make them available on the open marketplace exchanges. The combined point being that fake traffic is ubiquitous on the internet and comes from sellers of that traffic as well as some publishers who may be actively seeking it.

And for years open exchanges gave media buyers access to a glut of on-line inventory at rock-bottom CPMs. Buyers were always aware there was an element of waste in the supply; a few impressions that perhaps didn't quite hit the target. But with access to such cheap media who was really worried about a few wasted ad dollars? Since then, the real and hidden costs of buying into a bottomless market of cheap programmatic inventory have become apparent.

But what can marketers do to avoid being duped by unscrupulous publishers?

Beyond using the best verification tools, advertisers and their agencies should have standardized ways of working with selected partners to deter-mine what those partners are putting in place to ensure quality sources. Align on what verification technology any publisher partner is using, and pose the right generic questions:

- "Is your property purchasing any off-site traffic drivers?" Publishers will experience higher IVT rates if they're purchasing non-organic traffic.

- "Do your properties have ads.txt and robots.txt implemented?" Having an up-to-date "ads.txt" file on their site will give you greater control over their traffic and help to prevent bad actors from being able to counterfeit their inventory.

- "Are you checking IP addresses for known bots?" There are services available that are capable of checking traffic's IP addresses against known bots in the space to limit known non-human traffic.

If you're an advertiser, asking the right questions and using the right verifi-cation partners with granular datasets will get you in a good spot. If all you get is one number from a verification company's report, you can't trouble-shoot anything with that. But if you have a list of sites and apps that are cheating, you can add them to blocklists or remove them from your inclu-sion lists.

And if you are one of those publishers who may be exposing themselves to invalid traffic because part of that traffic is bought, then stop sourcing cheap remnant inventory from dodgy sources.

IDs and crumbling cookies

Cookie IDs have been the backbone of identifying individual users almost since they were introduced in 1994. Initially just a means of making sure that users didn't have to continuously update their shopping carts, their role expanded, and they have become the bête noire of the era of privacy.

With regulatory pressures around protecting consumer privacy, it's no accident that the industry is having a bit of a flap around the viability of cookie-based measures. Some, but not all, verification technologies have been dependent on them.

And advertisers fear that they are on the brink of losing their overall ability to measure advertising campaigns with no industry consensus about what to do next.

"If we don't diversify our approach to the market, soon we'll be operating by the equivalent of candlelight. Over two-thirds of advertisers are not revising their measurement strategies" (IAB, 2022).

These are the types of statements you can hear off-stage and in the corners of the coffee area at most advertising conferences.

We are regularly asked questions by clients, investors, prospects, and industry committee members about how brands can operate in a cookie-less environment. As the industry attempts to wean itself off reliance on tracking cookies, the number of different understandings of what will actually happen is too damn high! This is not surprising, given the variety of interpretations in the trade press and wider technology reporting.

Macro-targeting of audiences will still be effective, and has been proven for decades with magazines, newspapers, and TV channels. The obsession with micro-targeting, which cookies facilitate, in many ways has only fueled surveillance behaviors and it can only be a good thing to phase it out.

The fact that most internet users now have to live with consent pop-ups at an unprecedented scale has only highlighted what cookies do. These pop-ups are also indicative of just how sneaky the industry remains.

Most cookie consent pop-ups tend to reference the usual things in terms of flagging whether the tracking is accepted in for example, "selected basic ads," "creating a personalized ad profile," "creating a personalized content profile," "measuring ad performance," and "measuring content performance." Normally and correctly these boxes for each are left unticked in terms of open consent. But if you look a bit closer, all the same items, and all the same associated vendors tend to be pre-ticked for the same types of consent, but on a "legitimate interest" basis, in the largest hidden tab. It's akin to consumer cookie consent by stealth, and still happening today at scale.

"Legitimate interest" in use of tracking data, combined with the IAB's Transparency and Consent Framework (which we will touch upon later), have been the questionable life rafts that the cookie-based industry has been holding onto post-GDPR, pre-Google cookie phase-out.

The industry has been frantically making noise about cookies for some years now. Table 1.2 shows a few fundamental misunderstandings, based on what we've seen, together with some sober clarifications for each.

"The cookie is crumbling" is likely to be the most overused line of the last couple of years and has become something of a cliché. Neither advertisers nor publishers need to fear the changes. This is going to be a strategic shift, just like many of the others between 2015 and 2020, like Apple's Safari browser stopping third-party tracking, and will be addressed.

Table 1.2   Common cookie "manias" and some measured corrections

Common cookie "manias"	The reality
1. "All cookies are going away."	Third-party cookies are being phased out of Google Chrome (80 percent of users).
2. "Cookies have been the foundation of targeted advertising and are the crux of digital efficiency."	Cookies helped support more targeted advertising but are not at all a perfect tool for precision in online advertising.
3. "Frequency caps will be impossible."	There are emerging solutions to do frequency caps per publisher or supply source (first-party data is still able to be used). But not always across sources. This is as much as was possible all along.
4. "Ad budgets are going to shift offline."	Ad budgets go where the eyes and ears are, and that is still increasingly online.
5. "The responsibility to find and create new identity solutions will be on advertisers and publishers."	The adtech tax (the amount of budget that goes to intermediaries) as we will later outline is circa 55 percent! Let adtech earn its keep.
6. "Google is deciding exactly what happens next."	Chrome is run by a different team within Google, and the ads team is still proposing alternative solutions to targeting without third-party data usage.
7. "Publishers fear that their RPMs are going to drop."	Ad budgets will remain online, and this is an opportunity for RPMs to increase with fewer middle-man fees.

Table 1.2   (Continued)

Common cookie "manias"	The reality
8. "'Workarounds' are still unclear, as are privacy sandbox specifics."	There are several pending legal challenges and government regulatory processes that can significantly change the roll-out and direction of these policies.
9. "Google and Apple changes are punitive toward the advertising industry."	This is very far from the truth. Advertisers are the primary customers of Google, and a big consideration for Apple. But these policies are about the user, not advertisers or publishers.
10. "Ads will not be relevant to the user, negatively impacting experience."	Our perception of "relevant" is key. When you are on a food blog and an ad for a product that could be used for the recipe is shown, is that relevant? Yes, and actually it is a contextual scenario. It feels personal but it's not "personalized." When you leave an e-commerce site and are served a banner for a product from that site 18 times in a row, Is this relevant? One could argue yes, but then add, "annoying"—and that annoying has led us to privacy issues.

The particular shift that the industry is going through right now is a fantastic opportunity for advertisers to re-evaluate how cookies and individual identifiers are used in their ad strategy. It is also a great opportunity for publishers to realize again the true value of their audience, rather than the auxiliary targeting technologies that chipped away at publisher revenue.

Anyone holding the belief that cookies and device identifiers were the key to advertising effectiveness should remember that the industry-wide click-through rate has until now been 0.01 percent (1 out of 10,000), which is a metric that includes bot traffic that amplifies click activity. Not to say that clicks are the holy grail of effectiveness, but it is one of the primary metrics used by advertisers and agencies.

There's no need to stress about third-party cookies not being usable if you don't really rely on them to begin with.

Privacy by design

Proper privacy-friendly ad measurement can assuage a lot of the concerns about what the effect of this will be. Being able to keep track of what ads get served where, and through what paths, is key to maintaining effectiveness. And this can be done safely and in line with the requirements that have been born of GDPR legislation in the EU, and all of the other national and state-based initiatives that have followed.

User privacy has been on the agenda of every advertising and web technology discussion since GDPR was announced and rolled out in May 2018. This has been further reinforced with the emergence of state-based laws in the United States (e.g. CCPA, the California Consumer Privacy Act). Privacy advocates had been ringing the bell for many years, and the legislation passed by the EU Parliament represented a regulatory watershed that popularized the topic in the thoughts and minds of non-industry folks and governmental authorities around the world.

User privacy and data security have become focal issues for the digital measurement industry. Ours too—as one of our own first priorities in 2018 was to devise a verification measurement product based on a methodology that is future-proof regarding sensitive PII (personally identifiable information).

Monitoring and tracking user behaviors is increasingly unsustainable and existing approaches that track, monitor, or "fingerprint" will be increasingly privacy-challenged. There is a growing need for a long-term approach to measuring and recording the data points relevant to ad transactions and their associated quality metrics that can meet ever-evolving privacy law requirements.

Beyond the verification space, "unique user identification" remains a big challenge in an emerging environment with no third-party cookie usage and widespread PII restrictions on data collection. Relying on sensitive PII and cookies is unsustainable and indeed often inaccurate. Even basic things like estimating the gender of online users were only correct 50 percent of the time.

There are ongoing attempts to resolve and replace these cookie-based signals as a basis for ensuring uniqueness of users, for the purposes of accurately reporting vital marketing metrics like reach and frequency, and it remains to be seen how potent and indeed legally viable each will prove to be.

There are alternative approaches out there. One study shows that "GPU-based fingerprinting" can be more effective, but also potentially fraught with privacy concerns. This is where the unique characteristics of the device you are using can act as a surrogate to ID you. For example, one (Laor et al, 2022) is a methodology based on GPU (graphics processing unit) measurement that was identified by a group of academic researchers as the next phase of user fingerprinting online. It focuses on the unique signatures associated with certain bits of a device like graphics cards. But the discoverers of this methodology themselves have concerns that this will be used for surveillance and persistent tracking.

Device-based versus people-based measures

Tracking and classifying people is therefore increasingly off-limits. And many would agree that it is about time. And the fingerprinting example above is one of an altogether different kind of approach.

The future of some measurement is increasingly device-based, particularly verification and event tracking. Being reliant on the "native" elements of devices, versus any user-based identifications, has the regulatory advantage of being privacy-friendly and the operational advantage of being difficult to spoof.

Native device properties are fundamentally required for browsers, apps, and other content servers to properly deliver and display content to users. Attempts to enable spoofing of these types of properties have been stopped by developer administrators at major browsers (MMI, 2020).

We have found that a device-based approach is the perfect antidote to increasingly privacy-challenged approaches to verification measurement. This approach fulfills several ongoing industry privacy and operational challenges simultaneously:

- not being reliant on cookies or sensitive PII;
- using native characteristics of devices provides objective, quality measurement as they are nearly impossible to spoof;
- being able to establish user uniqueness within the parameters of data privacy frameworks.

Additionally, a device-based approach helps partially solve the industry-wide reliance on probabilistic-based data science and associated sampling techniques. The "universe" of bots on the web is evolving and growing.

Companies such as Imperva, Barracuda Networks, and others have completed research that independently confirms over 50 percent of overall web activity is non-human initiated. This number will continue to grow in the coming years, limiting many data science or anomaly detection-based approaches.

With scaled measurement of events with device, not people, classifiers, there should be less of a need to rely on sampling and data science methods to fill knowledge gaps. At least in the verification space. For wider measurement ambitions we recommend working with your partners to devise broad frameworks. But verification is also foundational to these other workstreams. Removing non-human users is foundational for general enterprise web analytics and for reporting reach, frequency, and uniqueness in an increasingly web-based ad delivery market.

If your organization is leaning toward using a workaround that replaces cookies as a unique user identifier, you are not necessarily going to have a good time anytime soon. But you don't need cookies if you are measuring and validating the quality of transactions rather than users.

As auditor consultants from 2016 to 2019, we analyzed the log-level data (receipts) of over a dozen large advertisers and holding company agencies, and found that even with the unique identifiers designated by the bidding technologies, true ad delivery was 20 to 30 times the designated frequency cap.

There is already clear evidence that the methods used in the verification and auditing space need continual refreshment. Sometimes these tools don't do what they say they do.

There are types of fraud, and different techniques within those bucket types.

Put very broadly, you can fake 1) audiences, 2) content, and 3) actions. The types *that require the least amount of effort* are, not surprisingly, the most prevalent. And some of those very prevalent ones are spoofing the industry at scale.

In one piece of research that was the precursor to some of our ongoing workstreams, 100 percent fake bot traffic was sent through the system to see how many verification suppliers would catch them all.

It was like a mystery shopping exercise, but with bots. One of the leading suppliers of bot monitoring technology proudly said "15 percent are bots," another said "35 percent." Both of these companies are global leaders in their field. This was the research conducted for a paper titled "Mystery Shopping Inside the Ad Fraud Verification Bubble," which became a foundational learning in the formation of MMI's measurement approach (Dhar, 2016).

The domain used for the research was www.ecelebnews.com, and for nostalgic and slightly sentimental reasons, the registration for this domain has continued to be paid since the paper was released in mid-2016, although the content no longer remains. The domain featured four pages of plagiarized content from an entertainment news and gossip newsletter—unoriginal and scraped, with fake traffic.

And within five business days, it was approved to run ads by a major ad network connected to the primary exchange marketplaces. The barrier to entry for the system to avoid being gamed was non-existent.

The experiment was intentionally run in a rudimentary fashion by clunkily sending page visits to a site that would then load the third-party ad requests. It proved quite artless in generating more revenue from the ads than was being spent on sourcing the traffic.

There were over 1 million visits to the site, and many millions of ad impressions generated, but the page analytics only registered screen resolutions for under 2,000 visits, 1,500 of which were declaring 800×5000 pixel displays. Having intimate knowledge of the source of the traffic, it was known that the operation ran automated browsers in data center-based cloud environments. All of the traffic was fake.

Two of the market-leading bot detection technologies only detected under 50 percent of this fake traffic, while those with much less market share detected up to 90 percent of the non-human activity. All four of the bot detection technologies involved used their own proprietary models to classify bots that changed over time as new data was processed.

It was extremely counterintuitive at first that those verification companies with the largest market share were less effective at bot detection. The ah-ha! moment came when the dots were connected to the availability of "pre-filtered" traffic designed to pass specific detection systems at 95 percent success rates. Being a market leader had the curse of becoming naturally less effective and accurate. The longer the tenure on the throne, the more exposed their methodologies became to those wishing to game the system.

Overall, bots seem to be winning. They don't just load pages and ads, but consume media (video and audio), inflate streaming counts, scrape content, and purchase limited-inventory items and experiences (like tickets and sneakers). The bot problem has now definitively grown to a point where it is not just negatively impacting businesses in a financial sense, but also negatively impacting human consumers in a social sense by creating distrust and artificial price barriers between them and their desired goods and services.

At MMI, we are proud to have built a solution and a company that helps advertisers make objective decisions at scale, in the most complex scenario, a 50–100 millisecond ad transaction window, while maintaining user privacy and data safety compliance.

Bots are also a moving target. There are plenty more solutions waiting to be built that cover emergent threats to serve the companies wanting data hygiene and reliability. We do not need to be afraid of bots, as there is so much wonderful web technology, like search engines, that relies on good bots.

But we are at a critical point in the history of the internet, where at any given moment, there is one bot program running for every human active on the web. It is up to us to make sure we can tell the difference between human and non-human activity, so that the next 20 years of internet growth and development are founded on reliable, trusted, and sustainable metrics. It at least demands open and honest dialogue with agency and platform partners. And in order for that to happen, we need to build a common language.

The efficacy of all types of measurement methods across the board, from audience measurement, through to verification, and even outcome measures… is, to put it politely, a shit show. And this has been happening at a time when partners, like auditors, who were the traditional, quality-assurance gatekeepers in the industry were asleep at the wheel.

Many brands understand that their historical media audit programs have become an outdated game. Legacy pool-based media auditing is finished. With over half of media bought in biddable environments, there is more data across more advertising spend than ever before. Pools have become smaller, shallower, more unhelpful, and in many cases irrelevant. Legacy auditing dined out on pricing opacity, encouraged a race to the bottom on price, and measured brands against the same limited metrics. But this does not mean that independent auditing and governance are no longer required. Far from it: media auditing is now more important than ever given marketers struggling with complexity and the specialist skills required to assess the recommendations made to them, a higher risk of error and wastage to be mitigated, and an industry talent drain leading to less experienced and in some cases under-resourced agency teams, stretched across more clients and activities.

Whilst it was always obsessed with "cost versus quality" assessments and trade-offs, the nature of the metrics involved now covers an expanded range of quality metrics to include IVT, viewability, brand safety, and in-geo determinations. All of them now need tech partners to achieve this.

Marketers have never been great at admitting knowledge gaps, and the granular data that is now available to them should minimize this going forwards. Tonnes of it.

The dangers of too much data

Yu, shall I tell you what it is to know. To say you know when you know, and to say you do not when you do not, that is knowledge.

CONFUCIOUS, CIRCA 500 BCE

Does more data lead to better decisions, or worse decisions? Especially in the current context of floods of available datasets, all marketing metrics are imprecise to some degree or other.

Decision-making science tells us that having some data is generally better than having no data. A researcher once ran a study where a group of professional gamblers were given increasingly more data, while continually measuring the accuracy of their bets. What they found was that having some data is generally better than having no data. But after a certain point, giving a gambler more data will actually decrease the accuracy of their bets, not increase it (Slovic and Lichtenstein, 1973)

Why is this? It's largely due to what can be referred to as the "signal-to-noise ratio." In any dataset, there is a signal (important information that you must heed) and noise (meaningless, distracting information). And, as a general rule, more data means more noise, not more signal.

So, what's the solution? The solution is to prioritize quality data over a long period vs. "big data" within a short period. Quality and time are what separates signal from noise.

And quality is not a subjective measure that should be determined by the specific beholder. But unfortunately, we inhabit an industry that is full of datasets that only serve the interests of the sponsors of that data.

"What makes a good traffic count good?" is not a subjective question. There are good sources and bad sources of truth.

As the saying goes, there is only one beautiful baby in the world and every mother has it. What makes a good publisher good is not akin to asking "what makes a baby beautiful?" It should be an objective measure.

Publishers and tech platforms cannot assess the veracity and quality of their own traffic counts. It should be left to independent auditors, measurement companies that can accurately overcome the challenges we have outlined, and the industry bodies like the MRC who police them.

There are a growing number of instances where publishers who have experienced exponential growth have been caught out when asked to verify the quality and sources of their traffic. Their downfall is an object lesson in the ubiquity of fake traffic, unnaturally sourced traffic. And marketers need to learn.

It's important therefore to bust a few myths and keep a healthy degree of skepticism when presented with other people's data. It can be politicized and inaccurate. Or just plain wrong.

The very idea of how an industry can falsely worship "digital data as the basis for personalization" is perfectly illustrated in the story of the "default IP address."

Butler County, Kansas is what you would picture if you imagined somewhere in the middle of the United States. Surrounded by the great plains, it is just south of the Kansas–Nebraska border.

It also just happens to contain the calculated geographical center of the 48 states in the main landmass that is the United States (excluding the likes of Hawaii and Alaska). It's "bullseye USA" for data and map geeks. Or "39°50′N 98°35′W" to be exact.

It's the kind of place that doesn't drive national news, but if something happens locally everyone knows about it. That something, or a series of somethings, happened to one local couple.

James and Theresa Arnold moved into their 623-acre farm in Butler County, Kansas, in March 2011. Over the next few years, they had countless visits from law enforcement authorities investigating a series of crimes. Tax fraud, stolen cars, stolen credit cards, even the illicit production of pornographic films. All crimes connected to this one Butler County farm.

Why was this? Either that location was a one-farm crimewave, involving a horrific concentration of events, or there was a systematic error that led to this family being falsely interrogated. Of course, it was the latter.

MaxMind is an IP geolocation analytics company. Many companies in adland rely on companies like it to help process and use one of the natural byproducts of all ad event "logs"—the IP address associated with an impression or click event.

IP addresses are of course the geographical identifiers that most of us will be familiar with. We all have one. Or a few as the case may be. It's a unique string or identifier of your access point to the internet.

Companies like MaxMind store and process and help connect IP addresses to wider datasets. Specifically, they provide geographical coordinates for IP addresses. Give them an IP address and they will tell you where it's officially registered. For the most part.

But IP addresses can be unreliable sources of information. They can be difficult to determine and locate and can even be spoofed. Because devices and locations can be victims of impersonation. No one was actively impersonating the farm in Butler County. What was happening was much more benign than that.

Companies like MaxMind know the ins and outs of geographically classifying IP addresses. Whenever they come across IP addresses that look particularly problematic to identify they put them in a digital "bucket." That bucket is simply labeled as the exact geographical center of the United States (or a convenient set of coordinates near that center). So, whenever a tech-savvy criminal was masking an IP address, MaxMind would classify the activity accordingly, and the location of that Butler County farm would pop up into the database. Which was then tapped into by authorities, with the resultant visits and raids to the innocent farm, day and night.

This went on for 15 years until the family took legal action.

Most digital ad verification companies rely on companies like MaxMind to facilitate a determination on whether a campaign ran in the region that it was intended for. As we shall see, the unreliability of IP addresses as an identifier is not the only part of the digital ad system that is prone to significant error.

What's old is new

We are living through a period in the industry when what was old has become new again. And the measurement game is not immune to this.

Digital datasets are being questioned, surveys are on the rise, and advertisers are revisiting those tried and tested techniques such as media mix modeling. Tried and tested approaches that have been in a state of flux, but their purveyors are taking the business.

Even Google is recruiting participants for an online panel and working with Gallup to build a tool that will serve as a benchmark to help validate the models that Google uses to estimate online conversions. Remember, Google is not a "closed loop" like Amazon where outcome attribution can often be deterministically measured.

"Panels," "models," "estimates." This is not the measurement nirvana we were promised but it is the one we are facing.

The "outcomes measurement" industry is going through a period of readjustment, some of it good and some of it bad, largely off the back of increasing restrictions on tracking and therefore attribution.

Things like "last click attribution" should thankfully disappear. It has dominated "return on digital spend" conversations for far too long.

Just because some communications channel or ad event happened just before customer conversion doesn't make it God-like. It was comparable to a striker in a soccer match scoring a goal, and then taking credit for the work of the whole team in getting the ball to the goalmouth.

Digital attribution, until relatively recently, was rarely connected to other datasets that would help contextualize the drivers of outcomes. And when it comes to cookies or user identifiers most marketers will be surprised by how little reliance there is on cookies for their company's ad and measurement strategy. In this space, overall, our advice to advertisers is to request a half-day with their agency or in-house teams to review how much of their advertising operation relies on third-party cookies and device identifiers like IDFA (identifier for advertisers) or AID (Apple ID).

So it's clear that "good signals" are ones that are 1) tied to clear goals, 2) have utility and purpose beyond simply being vanity metrics, and 3) are respectful of the legal and consumer demands associated with the era of privacy.

But in the basic counting and audience measurement games, and "media quality measurement" industry, there are some serious ongoing questions.

These are turbulent times for the usually stable and insulated world of audience measurement. There are a number of companies lining up to try and take Nielsen's traditional crown, with the likes of Comscore, Innovid, and others queuing up. There is growing pressure for cross-media measurement methodologies from the likes of the WFA and ISBA Project Origin.

And there are challenges around the industry's ability to monitor, control and measure the very nature of the quality of the supply of digital impressions themselves. We will cover this in the next chapter.

References

Dhar, S (2016) Mystery shopping inside the ad fraud verification bubble, Slideshare, https://www.slideshare.net/ShailinDhar/mystery-shopping-inside-the-adverification-bubble (archived at https://perma.cc/KD82-LR9X)

IAB (2022) State of Data Report 2022, https://www.iab.com/wp-content/uploads/2022/02/IAB_State_of_Data_2022_Master.pdf (archived at https://perma.cc/P3BE-KLR7)

Imperva (2021) The Imperva Bad Bot Report 2021, https://www.imperva.com/blog/bad-bot-report-2021-the-pandemic-of-the-internet/ (archived at https://perma.cc/4BNB-J4TD)

Laor et al (2022) DRAWNAPART: A device identification technique based on remote GPU fingerprinting, *HAL Open Science*, https://hal.inria.fr/hal-03526240/document (archived at https://perma.cc/33TP-6LHL)

MMI (2020) In Plain Sight: How developer tools enable invalid traffic, https://www.methodmi.com/reports/in-plain-sight (archived at https://perma.cc/QCY5-JRUD)

Slovic, P and Lichtenstein, J (1973) Response-induced reversals of preference in gambling: An extended replication in Las Vegas, *Journal of Experimental Psychology*, **101** (1), pp 16–20, https://psycnet.apa.org/record/1974-10382-001 (archived at https://perma.cc/6CQK-PN5R)

The digital supply chain

References to product origins have always been a potent part of the marketing messaging toolkit: *"Made in France/Italy/the USA"*... be that Burgundy, Milan, or Detroit... or any other place with appropriate product-relevant credentials. They each have their own particular and powerful associations, evoking original, historical, often mystical sources and production techniques.

Stamps of authenticity. Of, as the French themselves would say, *provenance*. Quasi-guarantees of tangible quality, reinforced by great product experiences. The very essence of powerful brands.

Particularly true of course for luxury brands, dependent on references to the *terroir* of the pinot grape, the design skills of the Milanese, or the skillsets found within the perfumeries of the Champs-Élysées. But a technique not solely limited to that sector. The building of *everyday* brands is also dependent on fostering associations and attitudes in the minds of consumers and backing that up in the real world. Because all strong brands exist in the mind of a consumer, as much as they do in your shopping basket. Perceptions of their quality are often the precursor to them dropping onto your wish list in the first place.

Advertising at its best has always worked in this space—playing with, eliciting, and creating new intangible associations that can be backed up and made real through physical experience.

It's an industry full of craft skills. As much about psychology and chemistry as it is about math and physics. A balancing act between expectations and experiences, the imagined world and the real world. Playing on notions of provenance and scarcity, for example—easy wins in the space between these intangible and tangible worlds for any traditional marketer—is as critical as it ever was. With the 21st-century consumer only becoming increasingly particular about quality perceptions. But with one critical addition from that consumer perspective, namely... *what kind of supply chain is involved?*

New awareness of "supply chains"

As consumers, we are increasingly demanding particularly new types of proof and verification. Extra information about sources and supply chains. Some validation that companies not only "say things" but also "do as they say." A degree of transparency not previously sought. *Corporate social responsibility* made manifest in their brands. Where corporate governance meets marketing.

"Cage-free eggs," "free-trade coffee," "grass-fed beef," "organic strawberries": As any trendy, foodie friend in a posh restaurant might tell you, "I want menus that are clear, informative but also evocative." They tend to be the types of people that go for "a low-carb mousse with avocado from the hills of Central America infused with cocoa from the Ivory Coast." Which can look like a pile of poop to others (who might have already tried mixing avocado and cocoa powder). Others might exclaim, "I just want to try good-quality, great-looking, fresh food... I don't always want to know its full personal history or its CV."

Outside of the industrialized world, when scarcity is rampant or when basic priorities are fundamental, "just having" is the prerequisite. Only during significant social and economic crises does the industrialized world revert to such drivers. It's no surprise that the onset of the pandemic of 2020 was associated with a fundamental recalibration in this regard, a year when the global personal luxury goods market imploded (Kearney, 2022).

But when abundance is the norm, consumers with elastic budgets and disposable income seemingly prioritize not only quality over quantity, but also the intentions of the brand and corporate *purpose*, and the everyday behaviors of the holding companies in question. Inclusive of the ethics of their suppliers providing the raw materials.

Great companies and their brands increasingly depend on this combination of evoked imagery and control of supply chains. Quality control of inventories is not only critical for production, but the bedrock of an array of modern advertising messaging. Digital or otherwise.

If consumers are increasingly asking for references to the provenance of products, brand marketers are, and to some degree always have been, attuned to it. With the great supply chain crisis of 2022–23 playing out before our eyes, brands are leaning into it because they know that managing physical and mental availability is critical to success. Responding to new supply chain demands operationally and continuing to message in line with a growing consumer base focused on ethical and corporate supply chain responsibility. In short, great business governance.

Which begs the question, why are many of the very same advertisers so awful at controlling their own digital advertising "inventory"? More critically, how good are their media buyers when it comes to the "provenance" of the commodity they themselves solicit... human attention? How do they behave given their own new digital supply chain in this new digital "attention economy"? Are advertisers and their agencies themselves as discerning as their customers when it comes to how they source and select digital traffic? When budgets are large, do they "prioritize quality" and the "responsible sources" of that attention? Where and how does that great business and brand governance meet *digital trading*?

The commodities of digital trading

Revenue generation, be that reaped in the short or long term, remains the ultimate goal of most marketing investments. And digital advertising investment can either be seen as a cost associated with short-term performance goals, or an investment related to longer-term aims.

By its very nature, digital activity produces a plethora of metrics, some of which are directly related to overarching revenue goals, and others little more than "vanity metrics" that look good on a dashboard.

Only a few of these, though, can be considered *currencies for digital trading*. "CPM" (cost per mille) still remains the metric of choice with which to transact digital media. Which in essence is comprised of two things:

- a measure of cost (usually expressed in US cents);
- a measure of human exposure (usually expressed in terms of thousands of "impressions").

Hence the cost per "mille" (or 1,000 impressions). Which in and of itself begs the further question, what exactly is an impression? A question which, on the face of it, should be easy to answer. But this is digital advertising; there are more terms and definitions than you can shake a virtual stick at.

As outlined in previous chapters, "impressions" represents a flawed but useful basis for a trading currency.

There have been numerous attempts to create currencies beyond CPMs. Some are based on specific types of audience, and others attempt to put in place cross-device, digital and non-digital metrics (an example of the latter being Project Origin).

None of which are, as yet, nearly as pervasive as CPMs. And that indeed reflects the very nature and power of a trading currency versus other metrics that drive other sides of the business (like strategic planning or insight generation).

Regardless of a currency's utility beyond basic trading, the pervasiveness of it is powerful. Shared assumed values, and common standards, are difficult to budge.

So "impressions" remain the basis for trading in an industry with circa $300 billion traded annually using them as a foundation. But they are not static, nor unchangeable. Different parts of the supply chain have different counts. They are intangible and fluid. Not exactly akin to traditional notions of stocked-up and available "inventory."

George John, founder of RocketFuel, said notably in 2010, when programmatic digital ad buying was being compared to high-frequency trading in the stock market, that "Impressions are more like snowflakes than stocks. Each one is unique and then they melt, disappear" (John, 2010).

His remark cut right through the confusion of the well-intentioned interviewer, pointing out the deep conceptual disconnect between what was being transacted versus how those transactions were facilitated. Targeted advertising whilst attempting to be unique to each individual user's experience and browsing profile, is also inherently impermanent and ephemeral by its nature. It's the ticking clock of impermanence that contributes to the complexity of counting these impression events across multiple servers.

Variable billing mechanics

This, in and of itself, leads to different cost calculations, depending on how you are charged, the point at which impressions are counted, and the basis of your billing.

"Billable events" are usually contractually very clearly defined, if often misunderstood. The two prevalent forms of charging are as follows:

- counts based on "bids won" (where, e.g., a DSP (demand-side platform) bills an advertiser on when they win an auction);
- count on download (where an impression is not counted until the user's client browser or mobile device sends back a ping that the ad has started to download from the ad server).

These are fundamentally different events, which happen in fundamentally different environments, yet are often conflated.

Any confusion here can cost you circa 10 percent of your digital media budget off the bat. Because DSP counts (happening in the cloud between systems involved in bidding mechanics) are often 10 percent or more than any impression counts happening related to content delivery. If you are not being billed based on completed and rendered ads on a web page, you are open to a chunk of your cash completely evaporating. For no good reason.

Watching your contracts is a good thing at any time. But understanding these billing mechanics could save you money up front.

These variable billing mechanics, combined with variable core definitions of impressions, combined with an ecosystem rife with bots… all mean that there is a plethora of nooks and crannies where waste can thrive. And given that all of this is happening in milliseconds, at scale, you can get a sense of where discrepancies can happen, and trouble brews.

There exists an industry tolerance for such discrepancies, largely based on a mutual understanding of the counting differences outlined above. Most buyers and sellers accept that DSP counts will differ from ad server counts by that factor of 10 percent or more. And other things like discrepancies can occur and are accepted based on, for example, technical issues between systems, or user-initiated behaviors like a web reader leaving a page before an ad is loaded.

What is more of a political hot potato is the fact that not all clients are actively aware of such things. And, more critically, there have been numerous studies that point to the fact that the "discrepancy" problem is much larger and more serious than what any buyer would tolerate or openly admit to.

Infinite intangibles

There is an abundance of supply in digital traffic, a bottomless well if you will. To give some context on the sheer scale of available inventory, the chart below compares the number of programmatically traded ad events per day with other types of transactions.

There are over 200 billion digitally traded ad transactions on a daily basis in digital advertising. This compares with 6 billion transactions on the New York Stock Exchange, and 1 billion credit card transactions.

Most of those NYSE and credit card transactions could be associated with some degree of discerning logic. A few, arguably not. Yet even the

Table 2.1   Estimated number of daily transactions per industry

Industry	Daily transaction count
Digital advertising transactions	200 billion+
New York Stock Exchange transactions	6 billion
Global credit card transactions	1 billion

largest buyers of ad space are not always particularly discerning about the quality of digital traffic. Mainly, but not only, because it's largely hidden from sight. A vast "fatberg of ad traffic" as one commentator put it (Manning, 2022).

The exponential growth in programmatically bought advertising has strangely coincided with a *perceived lack of trust in the quality of what is being bought*. As far back as 2014, the WFA (World Federation of Advertisers) itself reported that only 50 percent of global marketeers were confident that they were "getting what they sought" from programmatically bought ads (WFA, 2014). This lack of confidence has improved somewhat, but not to any extent that would help explain the goldrush that programmatic has enjoyed.

In fairness, that lack of trust in programmatically bought ads is still re-flected in the relative size of digital advertising that is, as an alternative, bought "direct" (or with greater awareness of what publishers and partners are targeted).

But for an industry otherwise steeped in the assessment of the quality of ad opportunities, an acceptance of leaky costs, inefficiencies and discrepancies does border on a lack of governance.

With low-quality ad traffic, the impact is not known or felt by default. Given the intangible nature of the commodity, the negative impact and consequences of buying low-quality ad space, even at a high scale, is largely a bit of a secret—unless the buyer is actively and consciously policing it. At the risk of oversimplifying how digital advertising success is measured, scales of volume and reach are the primary performance indicators for most initiatives. For media buyers, this type of success metric is simple enough as long as they can operate with a budget to match the aspiration. As one anonymous trader casually once stated to us, "all is good, the money is flowing."

The very notion of "inventory" itself is also a bit of an outdated concept for digital media. It denotes some kind of stationary collective of goods waiting to be sold, like cars on a dealer's lot or boxes in a warehouse. In the world of traditional printed media, newspapers and magazines were still able to reasonably use the word inventory because they knew how many copies were going to be printed while selling the ad space.

In the digital realm, however, the space is sold as it is even coming into existence with a page load, and then typically disappears altogether within a matter of seconds. With broadcast media, like AM/FM radio and traditional television, there were a fixed number of shows, with a fixed number of ad slots or placements, which resulted in a calculation of inventory that each network or show had to offer advertisers. Then came the layer of currency and value of those ad slots based on ratings from companies like Nielsen, Arbitron, and others, which allowed both advertisers and media owners to have an agreed-upon value of the audience based on reach and frequency of ad exposure.

This taxonomy naturally translated into the digital world because the organizations that purchased media, primarily agencies, were starting with a traditional media plan that just happened to include some digital buys and therefore operated under the same framework of planning and execution.

The difference in digital ads is that the ad slot or placement doesn't exist until the user actually engages with the content, and like a snowflake, melts and disappears as the consumer of content moves on to another page or site or app.

Troublesome cost transparencies

If the headlines are to be believed, there is an ongoing crisis of confidence in the advertising industry's ability to police itself in this regard.

A recent study into the level of transparency in digital advertising has referenced a "market riddled with material issues, including a lack of transparency in terms of data and dollars, fractured accountability, and mind-numbing complexity" (ISBA, PWC and AOP, 2020).

"Mind-numbing complexity" is not a great place for any industry to be. But that's where the ad industry, and particularly the digital industry, has found itself.

Adland and the traded commodities associated with it have gone through a significant revolution from the tangible toward the increasingly intangible. The proportion of spending going into digital channels is growing without pause. And the majority of this will be bought programmatically.

Table 2.2 Digital ad spending worldwide, in billions and total percentage of ad spending

	2019	2020	2021	2022	2023	2024
Digital ($B)	$325	$333	$389	$441	$485	$526
% of total	50%	54%	56%	59%	61%	63%

We will touch upon the evidence of long-term declines in advertising effectiveness later, and whether it is a direct result of these underlying changes in the types of spending. For the *efficacy* of marketing spends, the jury is still out on whether the drive toward digital media has been an inherently good thing. The answer being both yes and no, depending on who you speak to, what analysis period they have used, and how advertising effectiveness attribution has been calculated.

More critically, for the *transparency* around marketing spends and whether the rise of digital has been a good thing, it's a pretty damning "no." Because if there was a canary in the coalmine of digital advertising, in transparency terms, it was dead some time ago… the only surprise is that there hasn't been a demonstrable period of mourning, and little collective corrective action has been taken.

Study after study has tried to follow digital investment through an opaque market of intermediaries and madmen (reflected in both previous and ongoing ANA and ISBA studies). They have only succeeded in highlighting how money goes missing, and how much of each investment can be considered "working" (or in everyday parlance, for every dollar spent on programmatically bought digital media, how much of it actually gets into the hands of a media owner and buys a real opportunity for an appropriate consumer to see).

Previous and separate studies by the ANA, the WFA, and the ISBA have not only analyzed some of these issues but also reinforced several troubling conclusions, leaving the industry at a critical inflection point. In terms of monetary efficiency, taking these multiple attempts to unpack the digital supply path into account, one conclusion that has been currently reached, using multiple sources, is as follows:

1 You start with a dollar to spend digitally.

2 Your agency gets a 7¢ fee.

3 Technology (DSPs (demand-side platforms), SSPs (supply-side platforms), and targeting partner data) fees take another 27¢.

4 15¢ mysteriously disappears into an "unknown delta."

5 30 percent of the ads you buy won't be viewable (see verification partners like IAS/DV/MMI—see for example WFA, nd).

6 About 20 percent of what you buy will be fraudulent/non-human (verification partners like IAS/DV/MMI—see for example WFA, nd).

7 Only 9 percent of your display ads will be viewed by a real person for even a second (Lumen Research, 2021).

8 Your dollar effectively bought you 3¢ of real display ads viewed by real human people.

It's what one industry commentator has comically referred to as "the programmatic poop funnel" (Hoffman, 2022).

Granted, a lot of the above is relevant for a particularly troublesome part of the industry—the "open web display" portion of digital buying. But this is, ironically, the most measurable (and data-transparent) portion of web activity. At best, these numerous investigations (from the ANA, ISBA, WFA, R3, Ebiquity, AANA, and others) have demonstrated that only 40 to 60 percent of digital dollars programmatically invested by advertisers find their way to publishers in the form of working media and an audience ad exposure opportunity.

Cost-commodity-wise, there are few industries that would operate on these terms. But the sheer abundance of available inventory, its low apparent cost, lack of definitive evidence of ineffectiveness, combined with an ease of implementation, have led many to continue to spend. And not just continue to spend but to grow that spend. Exponentially.

Digital media now accounts for 59 percent of global advertising spending and will hit the mid-60s by 2023. This intangible digital supply chain alone represents more than $400 billion in global ad spend, larger than an array of national economies across the globe.

Direct and indirect sourcing

Direct buying of media is when advertisers work directly with a publisher to purchase advertising space on a website or in a traditional publication. It is bought via an "insertion order" (reflective of how "insertions" were bought in pre-digital print media). A price is negotiated, the placing of an ad chosen, as are duration and dates on which the ad will be shown to the publisher's readers. It tends to involve people talking with people. Almost a traditional mode of media buying.

Programmatic buying happens automatically through an ad-buying platform. The ads are bought and sold through an automated process managed through a piece of software with a dashboard.

In food terms, "direct" digital ad buys are like a good-quality steak, and "programmatic" auto ad buys can be like ground meat.

Burger consumers don't concern themselves with meat quality until they hear that it could be comprised of meat from 100 or more cows. In an ideal world, would you rather be consuming a fast-food burger made of meat from 100 different cows, or eat a single-cow burger at a restaurant down the road from a dairy farm? Milk and yogurt consumers don't concern themselves with the quality of the dairy supply until they think about how many different cows' milk was mixed to create their parfait or soften their tea or coffee.

Now if all the processes in those supply chains were diligent and properly enforced for the health and safety of the consumers, we would rarely see any serious issues. In the unfortunate scenario that there is an occurrence of Creutzfeldt–Jakob disease from consuming meat from cows with BSE (mad cow disease), it becomes exponentially more complicated to track back to which cow specifically from which place was the culprit. This complexity can result in literal tons of beef having to be recalled and taken off the shelves, causing a decrease in supply that raises the price of the remaining beef, unless weary consumers lead to demand falling enough to keep prices stable or even cause them to drop.

Ongoing approaches to digital advertising seem different. An industry where there have been consistent reports of fraudulent or non-human traffic in advertising supply, plagued with persistent opacities, and even documented corruption at large brokerage houses, the digital ad exchanges have never seen buyer demand drop out of caution. Even more surprisingly, they have not seen a drop on the audience/traffic supply side in any manner, meaning supply aggregators do not become more discerning on what traffic sources they allow to enter their marketplaces.

The programmatic lucky bag

People of a certain age, or those who still visit flea markets, will be aware of a natural marketplace phenomenon known as "the mystery bag." For those unfamiliar, it is in reference to a street-market trader who is trying to offload a mixed bag of items that remain concealed at an especially attractive price.

Flea-market traders still offer these mystery bags "full of unknowns for five bucks" at the end of a trading day, usually full of items that they couldn't otherwise sell. Remnant inventory. Often perishable things. Worthless through time. But still with a potential hidden promise, the "reveal" being part of the fun from any buyer's perspective.

In some global consumer markets, this was even elevated to being a branded product—for example, the *Lucky Bag* in the UK at one time was a mysterious branded packaged blend of sweets and toys. In truth it was used mainly as a way of getting rid of mis-shaped candy. Production anomalies. From the consumer perspective, though, it was fun while it lasted, largely because it was a known-unknown and there was a vicarious pleasure in watching others popping open their packet, not knowing what they would get. The problem was that the fussier kids got, the less they wanted them, and the brand declined and disappeared as a result.

To say that the digital advertising marketplace has, and continues to be, a bit of a "mixed bag" is an understatement. The digital advertising industry has been through an early version of this "mystery bag" phenomenon.

At one time, all digital advertising was bought directly. Programmatic buying, in its infancy, was initially driven by the selling of "remnant inventory" held by publishers that they were finding difficult to offload. Ad networks appeared to do this at scale—pretty much the mystery baggers of their time. As the number of publishers grew exponentially (the number of websites and apps), there was a need to bring efficiency to the marketplace. Ad Exchange business appeared to fulfill this need, sitting between those systems that helped buyers make buying choices (DSPs), and those systems helping sellers make selling choices (SSPs). Providers of ancillary services (like data provision and traffic verification) became extra add-ons, all focused on bringing a degree of certainty to what was otherwise a lucky dip. Which in essence is what remains today. A cast of intermediaries and pieces of software in a patchwork quilt of an industry, with a complexity that gives at least an impression of governance.

The suppliers working in the open web over the last 10 years are a vast and varied number of AdTechs that have launched products that claim to make advertising work harder. The reality is that the main beneficiaries have been those AdTech players themselves. Many have gone on to major IPOs (initial public offerings), reaping eye-watering financial multiples and using the proceeds to acquire other AdTech companies to keep the plates spinning before they cash out... like lucky carpetbaggers of the 21st century. Their "metaverse" and "Connected TV" are the equivalents for today, emergent on the wings and full of promise, with many commentators thinking, *let's fix the existing advertising internet before we build new empires.*

Brand marketeers and industry associations are beginning to show signs of a comparable "fussiness," like those kids in the UK, initially enamored with their unknown Lucky Bags. After all, it is their money, and only their money, that fuels the industry. And they, and their trade associations, are increasingly leaning in.

An industry leaning in

In 2017, the person at the helm of some of the largest advertising budgets in the world (Marc Pritchard of P&G) called parts of the digital industry "murky at best, fraudulent at worst" (Pritchard, 2017). His then counterpart at Unilever, Keith Weed, openly called on some to "drain the swamp" (Weed, 2018). Mr Weed pointed out at an IAB industry leadership meeting that while technology companies had done much good, there were unintended consequences of that work that needed to be addressed. He even made it a point to say that the industry needed to redefine what is considered responsible business in the modern digital era.

The WFA, who represent around 80 percent of global ad spends, have since then released numerous reports, all calling for greater active transparencies. As recently as 2020 and 2021, other national trade associations (ISBA in the UK, the AANA in Australia) have run related investigations into the barriers and practices holding up greater transparency in the industry.

There seems to be no lack of evidence and intent, but somehow the industry lurches from one report to another, with little or no collective impact. Or, as one commentator put it, "the dogs bark, but the gypsy caravan trundles on."

The latest manifestation of an industry trying to self-police itself came in late 2021, with the announcement from the largest national association (the ANA, or Association of National Advertisers, in the US) calling for and commissioning a new study that aims to go further than previous ones to include platforms that have been somewhat immunized from previous studies. Results should be due within a year. Or two.

All of which are noble attempts to address a fluid problem. Which is part of the issue. Either because these studies are complex and time-consuming given the scale of data and legal complexities required to stitch together insights of worth, or, because by the time the industry picks up on the learnings, the landscape has changed. Or they remain largely ineffective because they are so limited in focus and don't successfully take account of those large tech players who have zero transparency built into their modus operandi, the "walled gardens."

Much of the digital advertising landscape, particularly the open-web portion, looks like a Heath Robinson-esque collection of AdTech providers. Walled gardens, such as Facebook, who work through an owned and operated business model with integrated technology, are open about one thing— their lack of openness.

In many ways, the emergent Era of Privacy associated with legislation like GDPR in the EU, and the CCPA (California Consumer Privacy Act) in California, has only accelerated this stance. Privacy has been weaponized, and often used as the basis for a lack of data sharing. Even if that data is not, strictly and legally, in breach of such laws, and even if that data would facilitate industry transparency efforts.

If the open web is rife with unnecessary complexity, then the walled gardens could be accused of deliberate obscurity. Only regulation can now address the hegemony of these big walled garden platforms, with the efforts of individual advertisers and associations potentially only making a marginal difference. But that's no reason to not try.

The measurement challenge

With a supply base that is simultaneously fleeting and infinite, it makes the measuring and oversight of the path of purchase an imperative foundation of any governance strategy. It is a bit strange that marketers and agencies spend significant amounts of their clients' budgets on verification technology while also not splitting out the results by supply path from the very beginning.

You might be wondering why there is a supply path, or even a supply chain, in the context of advertising on the internet. Most people who are not in the weeds tend to simplify the concept to brand, website/app, and user. It has been studied and documented for almost a decade that at least 50 percent of advertiser spend is taken by the technology layers that enable ad targeting and serving (the earlier-referenced ISBA report). A previous experiment by the *Guardian* found that in a worst-case scenario it received just 30 percent of the money brands invested, with the rest lost in the supply chain (Ice, 2016).

As advertising has moved to be primarily digital, albeit accelerated by the Covid-19 pandemic that kept huge swaths of people indoors in front of web-connected screens for two years, there has been a fundamental shift in the way that ad planning and execution has had to be approached.

With broadcast media, the audience was, supposedly, based on a representative sample of the census and taken as a given, with the *measurement* of reach and frequency of different pieces of content being valuable to both content owners and advertisers. Advertisers knew that ad breaks were often the opportunity for someone to get up and refill a refreshment, replenish the snack bowl, or visit the toilet, since they were in attendance for the content as the main attraction, not aways the ads themselves (the Super Bowl being a bit of an exception).

Hence, it was the *opportunity to see* the ad that was valued and transacted on.

With digital media and advertising, it is *served* directly to an internet user's browser or device. The delivery and counting of reach (and even frequency if done right) is now a given, but it's the *audience* that is now the elusive unknown, creating a growing fervor for some new technology to have its *Lion King moment* and be the solution for quantifying the "identity" of audiences.

And, in all honesty, "*audience*" is as outdated for the digital realm as "*inventory*" is, because not only does it not fit the original definition (*a group of people who have gathered to watch or listen to something*) but it is also founded on basketing groups of consumers together based on a fleeting set of identifiers as they consume, largely determined by a number of black-box methods. Audience definitions, the very basis of applied segmentation at a foundational marketing practice, has not made the leap to the world of digital without problems. Even assuming a content type-based affinity is often a mistake in the context of a wild and freely available internet.

There is no currency that is more important to measuring and indicating marketing success in the digital environment than the actual delivery of ads to a user's device. The optimization of that metric can only be realistically done by refining the supply paths through which an advertising campaign gets delivered to the intended content environment or user group.

While supply path optimization (SPO) practices can vary, dependent on what the buyers are optimizing for (50 million reach, 2× per day frequency, <20 percent fees, 95 percent viewable, etc.) most endeavors in this space are a bit of a mythical beast.

A bit like the Yeti itself. Many make reference to "SPO," but evidence of daily habits associated with it on the buy side is hard to find.

It involves not only measuring the quality of digital traffic, but also isolating the sources of the good and the bad, and doing so in a manner that directly leads to corrective action made at scale, working with measurement partners, making sure you have data access rights, and building your processes into everyday automated buying practice.

Validating digital traffic as human is only the first port of call in such efforts. But most stop there, often negating any potential progress from the real work to be done. Others, as we shall see, simply make direct deals with the supply side, claim to create mini walled gardens of traffic sources, and just call it "SPO."

Supply path mapping

SPO can be defined simply as making sure you, and your partners of choice, are efficiently maximizing the opportunities to source quality traffic—however you define "quality," be that:

- the table-stakes measures of quality in terms of that traffic being a human, with a clear opportunity to see, and in an appropriate context; or
- specific quality metrics associated with strategic KPIs such as targeted audience criteria, or cost goals.

SPO efforts often happen in a current environment awash with industry-wide initiatives already in place (such as IAB Ads.txt, Sellers.json), "bundled" buying habits still pervasive, and third-party verification measures already deployed. Which often leads to a "we don't need to change our immediate behaviors" and we "have it covered" mindset.

The industry's collective ability to properly optimize was brought into question by the ISBA/PWC/AOP study in 2020. The reaction to the study exposing the gaps and challenges in tracking spend across the supply path was both significant and international. It generated a huge amount of press coverage, numerous webinars and podcasts, some lively debates, interest from government and regulators, and even an internet meme (Reddit, 2020).

It shouldn't be considered "normal" that 51 percent of an advertiser's budget is used up before an ad appears, nor that only 12 percent of impressions can be traced, as the core findings illustrated.

Some of these findings matched previous work going back several years but that didn't make them any less eye-watering. It just shows that very little progress had been made, and there were persistent issues around corrective behaviors in the industry and some overarching promises associated with the advent of programmatic around measurement efficiencies and control that were demonstrably yet to be realized.

Commentary around the report was vast and varied. Some of it reflected some fundamental truths that had to be retold. A lot of it, to the frustration of the authors, focused on the tabloid-esque headline afforded by the "15 percent missing delta" (Chester, 2022). Which was basically saying, "we don't know what that is and can't find it." That's 15 percent of globally traded, open web programmatic.

This is not representative of all programmatic, and it was never intended to be so, but the real stories to come out of it were two-fold and largely a call to action for the industry in two areas:

1 The challenges with data access and data quality: "there were myriad issues with data access and data quality. From when the advertisers, agencies and publishers signed up in June 2019, it took nine months to gather the data from the tech vendors."

2 Compounding these challenges were different data definitions and taxonomies, and missing data fields: "some data was only available at an aggregate level; multiple date formats alone; and of course, no transaction ID to match an impression from buy-side to sell-side" (Chester, 2022).

There was also a post-facto regret that no measure of basic traffic quality (around e.g. non-human traffic) was included, but the available data didn't allow it. And without industry-wide protocols around data access and data quality, as well as efforts to manage data quality issues by brands and their proxies, the issues will remain.

But brands can lean in and see for themselves, and often make significant cost savings.

Improving your supply

In terms of an "order of operations" for digital advertising practice, the most successful and efficient organizations tend to go in this order:

1 Put in place a means of measuring quality at scale, and quantify the sources of fundamental quality (IVT (invalid traffic), viewability and in-geo).

2 Connect these quality metrics with sources of traffic and buying partner technologies.

These two first steps are imperative to an organization's digital success and buying ads on the internet, where even the sharpest buyers rarely acknowledge that supply is unlimited.

In order to achieve this, the advertiser has to follow the following advice:

1 deploy available verification trackers in the ad server focused on quality metrics (IVT, viewability and in-geo) for 100 percent of ad events;

2 utilize available partner event logs and macros to enable you to track and unpack the "messy middle" at scale.

This information can be used for trading reconciliations and media partner assessments across display, video, in-app/mobile, and can be inclusive of basic quality metrics like fraud detection, viewability, and the geographical targets of the campaigns in question.

Figure 2.1   The two basic steps for supply path mapping

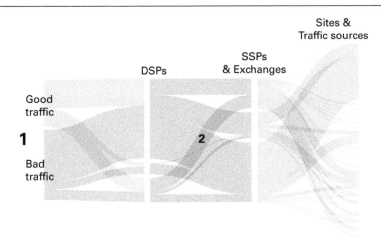

The basis of any supply path mapping is to essentially create and implement a mechanism to enable path changes based on quality thresholds.

If a certain supply path (DSP.1 × SSP.2 × Seller X) is under a pre-set viewability threshold of, e.g., 60 percent for 30 days, then it is time to direct that spend to another supply path (DSP.1 × SSP.4 × Seller Y).

SPO is akin to implementing railroad switches into automated ad buying at scale. The destination remains the same, but in order to avoid congestion, wasted time, added costs, and even collisions, the mechanical path is changed ever so slightly.

To make this a bit more tangible, we can delve into an experience from an actual measurement analysis we did for a global brand advertiser client. This travel-focused e-commerce company spent close to $1 billion just on digital ads across global markets. There was one agency of record for the buying of media, and this agency used a handful of technologies to execute the campaigns. One central ad server was the hosting repository of the creative assets intended to be served to users. Three to four DSPs (ad-buying platforms) were employed and connected to the central ad server, each with a stated unique offering based on targeting abilities, data partner integrations, optimization algorithms, and fee structures.

Now, from the buyer's perspective, it looks like they are running a transparent and straightforward media buying operation, with fewer technology invoices than fingers on a hand. Our team deployed a measurement tag into the ad server and collected data over one full month of activity.

Table 2.3 shows how reporting would typically look to a buyer like this.

While the DSPs are all bidding independently, they are all set up to target the same types of content and users because the goal of the company is the same: get people to come to their site/app and book airline tickets, hotels, vacation packages, etc.

Table 2.3   Example starting point for SPO

Platform	Impressions	Click rate	Conversions	Invalid traffic	Viewability rate
DSP.1	329,299,674	0.42%	152,339	5.66%	65%
DSP.2	207,119,541	0.21%	103,628	4.81%	70%
DSP.3	113,487,998	2.65%	205,741	18.3%	42%

There were many roads to the same destination, but each road tends to be associated with different "collateral damage" in terms of unwanted bots, bad viewability or other unwanted quality criteria.

Many roads to the same destination

There are indeed multiple, and often duplicate, ways to buy quality digital traffic.

A trend that is largely a function of two things:

1 the exponential growth of different types of digital platforms and traffic sources; and

2 some significant recent changes in the way in which digital inventory is traded.

Understanding these multiple ways to do the same thing, and the role of trading mechanics in the equation, is the core driver of what you should refer to as "supply path optimization." It comes as a result of doing the groundwork with measurement and data (not just as a result of, e.g., your agency doing a deal with a preferred supply source). Basically, making sure you are making the right choices when you are buying media, recognizing where there is a choice to be made, and taking ownership of it where appropriate and feasible.

Brands and agencies are faced with a plethora of such choices, with some available options more inherently transparent than others. The increasing prevalence of a trading mechanic called *header bidding*, which is a relatively new trading basis that attempts to democratize the availability of audience inventory, has had a significant impact on the duplication of the availability of that same inventory.

Put simply, you can find the same audience on multiple sources, those sources are making that inventory available to multiple buyers, and sometimes those buyers find themselves bidding for the same inventory whilst competing with themselves.

It has become more important for brand marketers to unpack where and when this happens, where the best sources of quality inventory are, and, critically, do so in a manner that helps them plan.

Like most things in digital advertising, "SPO" is having its moment, in column inches in the trade press, if not in practice. It is in danger of becoming not only a term that belies any daily habits on the part of agencies and trading desks, but increasingly a catch-all term that can be latched onto any industry initiative, sometimes falsely. Agencies are doing deals with specific SSPs and exchanges and calling it "SPO." DSPs are increasingly doing deals with specific publishers and dressing it up as "SPO."

Neither of these phenomena can be considered "optimizing" traffic from suboptimal and low-quality sources. Routing spends towards a smaller number of exchanges, for example, doesn't solve the issue *at source*:

- it demands a discerning buyer, with strong client backing, and good technology deployed at scale;
- brands should basically start taking control of these processes that use their own campaign trading data;
- agency initiatives that aim to "simplify the trading process and provide greater transparency" are in practice nothing more than restrictive deals;
- curated marketplaces may help improve the quality of ad exposure and cut the costs of transaction, but they are hard to scale;
- working with suppliers who offer full data transparency, within the confines of data laws, is critical.

Advertisers should recognize that programmatic media trading can work well if the right people and systems are involved throughout the executional chain, but very few advertisers know how to do this. They delegate responsibility too readily and lose sight of the advertising process too early, without the protection of audit rights and data access being built into their contracts. This can be avoided, and the better of the media agencies are showing the way.

The future will undoubtedly be dictated by the established, and some new, digital walled garden players. And advertisers will need to work with them in ways that are much more demanding of the platforms and provide better independent measurement of true ROI, but for this they will need new skills both internally and from outside their organizations.

In the meantime, they should learn how to get the best out of the open web and that means making it a far less opaque and much more accountable approach by truncating the supply chain, trading much more transparently, and measuring more accurately. This is all possible today. It's just not done regularly in practice.

Transparency traps

SPO is the new teenage sex. Everyone talks about it, nobody really knows how to do it, everyone thinks everyone else is doing it, so everyone claims they are doing it.

When pushed, everyone throughout the supply chain claims quality assurances are in place. Based on research we have undertaken with various national associations (AANA, ISBA) we tend to experience the following claims:

Brands: "Our agency are on it."

Agencies: "We use the best DSPs/managed service partners, practices, and verify."

DSPs: "We have the best algorithms, use the best exchanges, and verify."

Walled gardens: "We measure our own homework, it's a privacy thing."

SSPs/Exchanges: "Our sources are proven quality, and we verify."

Publishers and sources: "Our traffic is the best and organic/non-sourced, and we verify."

ALL: "We support the latest cross-industry initiative to drive change."

These are dangerous sentiments that often lead to inaction. If someone somewhere else is "on it" then there is no reason to lean in.

It's akin to assuming that some good folks over the hill are doing good things to defeat a scourge. Or conversely, if there are bad things that are happening, they are not happening here. And anyone who asks is faced with the classical retort that Lutheran missionaries faced in Sumatra in the 19th century when enquiring about cannibalistic practices... "that only happens in the next village."

Another dangerous mindset relates to some suspicion that opening the Pandora's box of transparency might not be a good thing. "Fear of finding out" or FOFO, as it has been referred to.

Others have claimed that too much transparency can be a bad thing. They cite that it can foster the very opacities it claims to cure (Bernstein, 2014), or that the excessive sharing of information creates problems of information overload and can legitimize endless debate and second-guessing of senior executive decisions (McKinsey, 2017).

But the accountability gap in digital advertising is glaring, and so pronounced that it would be difficult not to make significant immediate gains.

It's not an exaggeration to say that the promises of programmatic have not been delivered and sections of the market are both dysfunctional and hugely ineffective. Meanwhile the AdTech sector has become bloated and a source of untold wealth for some at the expense of advertisers.

The net result is that billions of ad dollars are being spent blindly. Lots of things have improved since the early days of digital trading, but a lot haven't. Maybe the worst kind of sentiment relates to what you often hear within the walls of the agency holding groups, that it's an "industry-wide" problem. A reason cited for inaction on a unilateral level. That is like climate change accepters not recycling because "everyone has to do it for it to work."

It is in advertisers' best interests to support the open web while they still can. It will decline over time, but the smartest advertisers will work out how to use the best parts that will endure while simultaneously developing an approach to walled gardens that makes them more accountable.

The truth may be out there but it's heavily disguised. So, protect yourself. The very act of leaning into transparency will foster a "Hawthorne Effect" (where the very act of putting supply path investigations into practice with your partners focuses minds and leads to immediate improvements in and of itself). As a final summary checklist before you do so:

- make sure you are clear on what impression counts you are being billed on;
- where possible use ad server counts as opposed to bid stream "impressions";
- have measurement in place for 100 percent of ad server impression counts;
- make sure you have data rights access to all counts in contracts (DSPs and ad server);
- recognize what behaviors agency-side will foster true "SPO";
- support industry-wide research projects that are focused on unpacking the supply path on both the open web and walled gardens;
- deploy supporting measurement technology that provides digital receipts for all ad events in measurable environments.

As practitioners in this specific space, we are regularly asked by advertisers to assess how buying partners are using available datasets and existing measurement workstreams to build better lines of audience supply. We have done so across three continents, worked with multiple agency groups, and been asked by advertisers, "Are we doing as much as we can in this regard?"

The polite answer is "No." We find a lot of campaign buyers who pay lip service to notions of supply optimization, but the reality is starkly mercenary. No one tends to exhibit the required daily habits unless they:

1 are asked by their clients to do so

2 have the tools and skillsets available to do so

3 are incentivized to do so

All of this is fixable now and we encourage everyone to lean into a space that will minimize fraudulent waste, reap immediate efficiencies, and maximize outcomes.

References

Bernstein, E (2014) The Transparency Trap, *Harvard Business Review*, https://hbr.org/2014/10/the-transparency-trap (archived at https://perma.cc/9AK9-2PDF)

Chester, S (2022) Stephen Chester, ISBA, interview with the authors, August 2022

Hoffman, B (2022) *Adscam: How online advertising gave birth to one of history's greatest frauds and became a threat to democracy*, Type A Group

Ice, B (2016) Guardian buys own ad inventory, only gets 30p to the pound, *Marketing*, https://www.marketingmag.com.au/tech-data/guardian-programmatic-advertising/ (archived at https://perma.cc/8Q94-RQSC)

ISBA, PWC and AOP (2020) Programmatic Supply Chain Transparency Study, https://www.isba.org.uk/media/2424/executive-summary-programmatic-supply-chain-transparency-study.pdf (archived at https://perma.cc/EP4Z-UNH8)

John, G (2010) You can't manage online ad inventory like the stock market, Venturebeat, https://venturebeat.com/business/you-cant-manage-online-ad-inventory-like-a-stock-market/ (archived at https://perma.cc/R49Y-KCYU)

Kearney (2022) Kearney Luxury Study 2021–22, https://www.kearney.com/consumer-retail/article/-/insights/how-the-pandemic-changed-the-luxury-industry (archived at https://perma.cc/JC29-LFQ8)

Lumen Research (2021) The Challenge of Attention, 2021, https://lumen-research.com/white-papers/the-challenge-of-attention/ (archived at https://perma.cc/7TD8-XYJ6)

Manning, N (2022) Advertising on the Open Web: fix it or lose it, The Media Leader, https://the-media-leader.com/advertising-on-the-open-web-fix-it-or-lose-it/ (archived at https://perma.cc/H8PQ-C3XT)

McKinsey (2017) The dark side of transparency, https://www.mckinsey.com/capabilities/people-and-organizational-performance/our-insights/the-dark-side-of-transparency (archived at https://perma.cc/6CD6-9DGQ)

Pritchard, M (2017) Marc Pritchard, IAB Annual Leadership Meeting, Hollywood, Florida, https://www.youtube.com/watch?v=NEUCOsphoI0 (archived at https://perma.cc/7M2T-9JFP)

Project Origin (2022) https://originmediameasurement.com/ (archived at https://perma.cc/5W4Q-7WGV)

Reddit (2020) Advertisers reacting to the ISBA/PWC report [r/adops] https://www.reddit.com/r/adops/comments/gfctrj/advertisers_reacting_to_the_isbapwc_report/ (archived at https://perma.cc/B47T-LMKJ)

Weed, K (2018) Keith Weed, Interactive Advertising Bureau's annual leadership meeting in Palm Desert, California, see https://www.cnbc.com/2018/02/13/unilever-tells-facebook-and-google-drain-the-swamp-or-lose-advertising.html (archived at https://perma.cc/PFJ9-PG2J)

WFA (nd) Digital Media Benchmark, https://wfanet.org/tools/digital-media-benchmark (archived at https://perma.cc/77RN-QRPV)

WFA (2014) Programmatic Media Guidelines, https://wfanet.org/knowledge/item/2014/07/03/Guide-to-Programmatic-Media-2014 (archived at https://perma.cc/4JRW-UNCC)

The skills gap   03

Advertisers may be spending money on media as if there's no tomorrow but about half of them have little idea if they're doing the right thing.

So went the headline from a recent survey from the 2021 WFA (Foster, 2021) whose members include the majority of global brands. Not one of the 52 respondents stated they were "very satisfied" with their ability to address the fasting-growing *revenue* source for global consumer businesses—*e-commerce*—with many looking for inspiration from sources outside of their industry.

The next largest gap was in the area of *measurement,* with a whopping 51 percent difference between the level of importance attributed to the topic vs. satisfaction with their own and their partners' abilities to address it.

The third-largest skills gap and area of concern—*transparency* in media trading—reported a 49 percent gap, with 91 percent of respondents emphasizing the importance of having transparency with only 43 percent stating satisfaction with their current capabilities.

Transparency, *metrics* and *money*. The three main areas that marketers themselves state as critical. But simultaneously, they are sometimes lost at sea when it comes to dealing with them. Which begs some natural questions: Is this a function of existing capability or team skills? And do those capabilities and skills reside in the right place? Within brands themselves, or within their agencies and partners, or the industry at large?

The generation game

Many of the advertising industry's current batch of leaders earned their stripes in the mid-1990s. A time when TV and print media were the dominant channels to manage.

That was when Mark Zuckerberg was about 10 years old, and Facebook still about a decade away. When Larry Page and Sergey Brin were just starting a student research project, which would evolve into Google. And Jeff Bezos had just left his job on Wall Street and moved to Seattle to register a new company called "Cadabra," which he then swiftly changed to "Amazon." "Abracadabra" might have been more appropriate, given that for the layperson at least, advanced technology can be indistinguishable from magic.

Between them, these three technology-driven companies, Google, Facebook, and Amazon, have pulled off more than a mere magic trick. They currently effectively own the global digital advertising market. Together, they now account for $7 in every $10 spent on digital advertising globally and are on track to absorb north of 60 percent of all monies spent on advertising.

As a result, anyone who is involved in media buying now and in the immediate future has to have the skillsets and mindsets associated with booking and managing advertising spends using specific platforms and pieces of software.

If not, can those people really say they "work in media buying"? Of course, they can. Especially if they work with the plethora of other tools that represent the long tail of media spending or are involved in other sides of the buying industry.

The point being, though, that many of the skills required to work in the sector today, and particularly media buying, are now *platform dependent*. The mechanics of how they work, and how they can be leveraged, remain a magical mysterious alchemy in the eyes of many current client-side senior marketers, who might still know the ins and outs of TV planning and buying from back in the day, long before they had iPhones in their pockets. They spoke a language of "flighting and frequency," and their media buyers one of "ad-breaks, rebates and lunch breaks." Many of them are now managing teams that are in the weeds of platform-dependent digital deployments, with "tags and image pixels," with "bid-streams and data segments."

The skillsets associated with media management today, like channel options themselves, have become fragmented and siloed.

But if the skillsets of the future are already here, they are just not evenly distributed. They are very specific to the platforms in question and marked by generational differences. And these generational gaps are most pronounced on the client side, hence the WFA research results, with agency-side leadership being at least bolstered by a continuous stream of 20-something digital natives.

The more things change...

A number of these skills gaps referenced are totally new, with not only e-commerce in ascendance but additional things not yet mentioned, like data privacy literacies.

Two of the gaps, though, have been around for decades—namely transparency and measurement challenges. It's just that they have changed their spots, and if anything have become more of a challenge given the number of platforms involved, and the rise of certain large platforms, some of whom tend to be transparent about their willingness *not* to be transparent.

As Matt Green, a director of the WFA himself, said with the release of the above-mentioned 2021 survey report:

> Media transparency has been a focus for the industry for a number of years and, while we accept that this is very much a moving target, it's disappointing to see that this still occupies so much attention from media leaders. These issues—old and new—require the client side to adopt new skills and they require renewed collaboration from across the industry. (WFA, 2021)

"New money and old problems" could be the tagline for the first two decades of digital advertising. Whilst much of this could have been anticipated, and acted upon, it's interesting to speculate why it hasn't. There may have been a fundamental expectation that transparency and measurement would have gotten easier. But here we are, in a transparency quagmire and a measurement mess. The tools of the digital revolution have not equipped marketers to change accordingly. Inefficiencies and effectiveness challenges are being addressed only as an afterthought, largely because measurement and transparency came only as an add-on, after the fact.

We are seeing this happen again before our very eyes. New media empires are being built off the back of zero measurement and no transparency. There is a rush to invest in Connected TV as the next-best digital channel in town. It is the fastest-growing channel in the US this year and primed to grow further, according to IPG MAGNA (Adgate, 2021). It will grow from circa $15 billion in the US in 2022 to double that in 2025 (eMarketer, 2022). Advertisers are queuing up to invest in it.

There is only one problem. Well, two. As we have outlined earlier, the CTV ecosystem has no full independent measurement, and there is next to zero transparency.

How can advertisers claim that they want more understanding of these two things on the one hand, whilst on the other hand giving billions to a part of the industry that palpably lacks the two things they seek? One can only assume that the two are connected, and there is a desire to fill the *industry-wide knowledge gap*. But it's not stopping the initial money flow.

And understanding why things like independent measurement of CTV platforms are a challenge demands some *familiarity* with the technology involved. As we will touch upon later.

The more things stay the same...

Media agencies, meanwhile, have been making hay whilst this opaque sun shines. As the old adage goes, "Give me the freedom of a well-designed brief... but a partially dysfunctional and ill-informed client."

Another perennial issue that has resurfaced as a result is the re-rise of self-reported metrics from media owners. Which used to be the scourge of the industry and "Rule number 1" if you worked in media research: "Do not trust or use media owner numbers." Independence of source is a virtue. Which leads us to "Rule number 2": "If you can't get independent numbers, then look for granular evidence and ask about methodologies."

Facebook, Google and Amazon themselves are famously reticent to over-share raw granular data in fear of, or thankful for, the shield of recent regulatory privacy mandates. And all sellers of digital traffic figures have their own proprietary sources of truth that often conflict with one another and never add up. Everyone is back in their own measurement "swim lanes" with very apparent technical and political barriers. Just brushing up against these barriers can invite uproar and defensive maneuvers, and the deployment of a random lawyer.

Any sellers of ad opportunities, with their self-reported metrics, cannot be considered independent sources of truth. Remember what was said in the previous chapter on the perishable nature of impressions, and supply chain discrepancies.

Leaders in both client- and agency-side organizations didn't "cut their teeth" in this new programmatic space. That's not to say that some of the perennial skillsets are now defunct, particularly the strategic and human ones.

But most digital diligence is delegated to junior team members, sometimes with insufficient internal training. The mechanics of trading has always been "juniorized" in adland, but never with so much inherent potential risk as now.

In the current climate, media buying should require a basic computer science education and technical awareness of basic internet mechanics. But recruitment into the media buying space is still largely focused away from the STEM (science, technology, engineering, and math) skillsets that suit. New recruits in the digital weeds of media buying are kind of thrown in there with minimal adult supervision. And often dependent on the training services offered by... the platforms themselves. Foxes in the henhouse indeed.

At in-person training sessions for demand-side platforms (DSPs), often the first thing a trainer will state to aspiring media buyers is to always be diligently cautious when inputting budget and spend-amount settings into the user interface, because there have been countless beginners who spent over \$100,000 in an hour that was intended to be spent over 30 days.

None of this is to suggest there is a high degree of sophistication required to operate methodically in this space, but we are strongly pointing out that the educational baseline in digital advertising must require more technical proficiency in web programming, server architecture, and the general structure of dataflows and structures on the internet.

Tech is eating your lunch

Part of the issue sits within the DNA of some client-side organizations, and indeed all of the agency holding groups. Agencies, and some advertisers, are not the home of cutting-edge technology.

At worst, many agencies have been described as nothing more than resellers of *other people's technology*. Indeed, many are incentivized by the tech behemoths themselves to act in this regard, with global deals being struck based on the number and nature of sell-ins to clients of a vendor's technology. And there are many case studies of campaigns that made a significant impact and difference to a client's business (which of course is a great thing), but when looked at in finer detail were the result of simply deploying the "Adobe suite" or the "Google stack."

Gone are the days when client-driven KPIs drove performance. Back with a vengeance are the days when media and platform owners, at least partially, help meet the underlying costs of running a media agency. It's only natural that staff members learn the craft associated with their ability to use a designated platform and function within their allocated specialism. They only become compromised if that sponsor is less than an independent arbiter of quality digital traffic, or if the tech landscape changes and makes those skillsets defunct. Both of which happen.

Programmatic practice is awash with "proxy" choices, otherwise known as getting other people to do stuff on your behalf. Some of those choices are of necessity because someone else owns the technology required.

On the other hand, some attempts to outsource tasks are driven by skillset issues, levels of knowledge, perceived leverage, resource constraints, and a multitude of other reasons.

All of course dependent on the task at hand, and often driven by expediency and commercial convenience, with recent brand efforts to "in-house" elements of programmatic buying well documented, ranging from simply owning the contracts, all the way through to having hands-on trading keyboards.

What if the task at hand is "getting greater transparency in the chain," what then? How is a brand supposed to behave, what are the things to look out for, what are the questions? Especially when it is apparent that they may be the only one with a vested interest in finding the answer? What questions should they ask of a buying partner and their partners in turn?

We will address these questions and offer operational frameworks for achieving and maintaining transparency in the digital supply chain in a later chapter.

DIY skills

Given this context, it is no surprise that client attempts at "in-housing" some of the requisite skillsets are trending.

Around 2018 there was a veritable frenzy of *in-housing* across many brands, and virtually every chief marketing officer had to spend time thinking about or having a conversation regarding bringing the media buying execution arm onto their own payroll in a specific department, or just keeping it with an agency with a commercial mandate to maintain reported efficiencies.

Like playing a board game with a group of competitive peers, the ones who understand and embrace the rules can succeed more than those that operate blindly. There's a difference between those who walk into a casino and take a seat at the table versus those that park themselves in front of a slot machine. One indicates some knowledge and skill. The other is somewhat more of a casual addiction.

That's not to say that those who never attempt in-housing are somehow lazy and bad. It is not for all and requires some fundamental prerequisites, which we will touch upon later. It is also a topic that inevitably ebbs and flows as a trend in the market. It is, at best, an effort to solve the underlying quality problems in the marketplace by solving the transparency problem for oneself at a very *surface level*.

It's very much an effort motivated by a desire to "take control." Or at least the illusion of control. It strikes one as curiously akin to the nationalist policy movements seen growing in many western electorates in the 2010s. The hubris of the UK prior to Brexit is indeed comparable to several brands that have tried and failed to in-house media. It also assumes that agencies have control of buying in the first place. If clients end up using the same tools that agencies use, it is a *transfer* of control. But no incremental gain is guaranteed.

In fact, when you ask around and look for highly successful examples of the in-housing of media, there are only a few. According to TPA Digital, a leading independent firm of digital consultants known for impartial advice, the most successful in-house efforts in the past few years in the programmatic sphere have come from brands like Expedia, HP, and Bayer (Blodwell, 2022).

A mashup of necessary skills

A trend that has been more pervasive, and this time with a lot more client-side relevance across the board, was the skillsets required to deal with the advent of the "era of privacy." GDPR in 2018, and the skills associated with the management and use of large sensitive datasets, became the cause-du-jour, and still remains so.

Data scientists, analysts, and engineers are a prerequisite to any kind of digital diligence. Fundamental to getting transparency, metrics, and money "right." And many clients have recognized not only their governance responsibilities vis à vis emergent regulatory pressure, but they have strategically understood the power and potency of their own datasets. Many would argue that this is the real leverage that any data-rich client has.

And of course, GDPR, and the follow-up privacy legislations like CCPA in California and others elsewhere, have been an absolute boon for the legal profession. A trend that has been sustained, with Data Privacy Law employment opportunities continuing to see record growth (TRU, 2022).

There was a period in the industry when legal headcounts doubled. New lawyers in the industry, whilst skilled privacy practitioners, had zero exposure to the mechanics of digital AdTech. They in turn had to be educated by digital traders on digital dataflows and partnerships.

A fragmented maelstrom of lawyers talking to digital media buyers talking to data scientists and software engineers. And these different teams didn't always play well together. In many ways an emergent skillsets mashup that was messy but necessary. And no one had a clue as to how the digital ecosystem could comply with GDPR.

The industry came up with a lifeline in the form of the IAB Transparency and Consent Framework (IAB, 2018). It was, and currently still is, the cross-industry effort to help publishers, technology vendors, agencies and advertisers meet the transparency and user choice requirements under the GDPR. Basically, it's the reason why those consent pop-ups appear every time you go to your website of choice. The framework was initially held onto with both hands by advertisers and their agencies and referred to as "best practice" by most when asked about whether their digital campaigning was aligned with the law.

A legal mess of biblical proportions

In 2022 it was declared illegal and largely unworkable by European courts (Lomas, 2022).

You couldn't make that up. It was a regulatory slap down for the industry trade body that positioned itself at the forefront of navigating digital advertising through privacy requirements. It was deemed in legal violation of things like *the lawfulness of processing; fairness and transparency; security of processing; integrity of personal data; and data protection by design.*

The industry remains in a state of limbo as to whether it is within the confines of emergent laws. Or not. For every AdTech salesperson with a great idea on how to deploy a campaign or leverage available data, there are now three lawyers to give 10 reasons why it can't happen.

Dodgy AdTech practitioners now refer to privacy "fanatics" who devised policies that get in the way of "practicalities." You might hear these practitioners say something dismissive to the effect of: "These guys are not privacy specialists; they are just anti-advertising."

But they are now a foundational part of necessary governance in the industry, and no one in the industry can operate without reference to in-house legal teams, as the industry awaits further clarity and enforcement of emergent laws.

There are conflicting views on what does and does not constitute private information in different territories. The use of IP addresses, whilst limited in terms of them being active identifiers, is prevalent. As are the use of content scrapers, which for the most part form the basis of the industry's effort to improve brand safety approaches. These verge on the illegal, depending on which lawyer you speak to at any given time.

Building discerning skills to measure quality

If anything, AdTech loves a mess.

Vendors have multiple solutions, agencies have white papers, advertisers don't know what's going on, and Google keeps ringing the cash register.

If you are an advertiser, and particularly a data-rich one, then there is a lot to be said for building upon your digital and data literacy skillsets, and embracing those verification specialists, fraud detection, and auditing companies who have no axe to grind other than ensuring that you and your agency are "doing the right thing and doing it well." In many ways, this basket of skillsets should be at the forefront of any (at least partial) in-housing.

Most marketers, though, have neither the computer science and web programming skills to deal with the intricacies of the digital advertising ecosystem, nor do they have the time. But at least learning the right questions to ask is within everyone's reach.

It's important to be able to raise the right kinds of questions about transparency, externally. Great brand-agency partnerships are like a successful marriage. Built on trust.

But like in any marriage, sometimes you don't just marry your loved one, but their whole extended family. In the digital ecosystem, this can take the form of third-party tech and data suppliers.

There are a number of key questions to ask any agency partner before you commit to a longer-term relationship. These questions help brands untangle the five areas which we consider the critical "order of operations" to help build trust.

Below is a handy list of those questions that you can ask of your agency and their technology partners. The answers to these will set you on the right path towards greater transparency, better metrics, and more money:

1 Billings transparency (what am I paying for?)

- Does your agency use any managed services to execute digital media buying?
- Does your agency bill clients for "auctions won" based on DSP numbers?
- Does your agency bill their clients for impressions based on ad-server numbers ("count-on-download")?
- Does your agency have a policy to disclose all mark-ups for third-party costs for data or verification services?
- Does your agency share any payment claw-back information (e.g. for invalid traffic (IVT)) with clients?

- In each of the DSP or platforms used by your agency, how many of your vendors offer you a self-serve platform?

- In the self-serve DSP or platforms, how many of your employees have access to all campaigns?

- How many of the DSP or platforms used by your agency only offer managed buying services?

- Does your agency ever act as "principal" in the selling of digital inventory?

2 Traffic validity (is it real?)

- Is third-party IVT detection deployed on 100 percent of impressions for all display campaigns?

- What is the CPM fee(s) for the verification vendor(s) used?

- What is the rate(s) of impression sampling used by this vendor(s), according to your agreement with them?

- Does your agency pick vendors based on their use of a third-party verification company that matches yours?

- Does your agency have a process in place to withhold payment to vendors for impressions verified as fraudulent?

- Does your agency suppress/black-list sellers (by name or ID) in ad exchanges?

- Does your agency account for data transparency when allocating budgets to vendors (i.e. domain reports or log files)?

- Does your agency employ a pre-bid detection filter on display impressions?

- Does your agency employ a post-bid verification filter on display impressions?

- For click-focused campaigns, does your agency monitor the landing page of the advertiser?

- For click-focused campaigns, does your agency monitor click drop-off rates?

- What methods are in place to address the inventory quality of in-app and CTV inventory?

3 Viewability (did it appear?)

- What is your standard for viewability that you guarantee for your clients?

- Are charges made for viewability services, and if so, what are the discrete CPMs?

4 Suitability and brand safety (in what context?)

- Does your agency maintain a domain "suppression list"?

- Does your agency add domains to the "suppression list" more than once per month?

- Does your agency run campaigns on a domain "allow list"?

- Does your agency update this domain "allow list" more than once per month?

- What methods are in place to monitor in-page content suitability and client brand safety?

- Are charges made for brand safety/suitability services, and if so, what are the discrete CPMs?

5 ROI (to what effect?)

- Do your agency vendors/tech stack partners tend to know a client's campaign goals?

- For analytics, do you maintain historical impression log files (receipts) available for your digital advertising campaigns?

- Are these log-level data files available to you with direct access or secondary access through a vendor/platform?

- Do you have a process in place to optimize the efficiency of spend/delivery on digital and programmatic ad campaigns?

- What data points do you use in this optimization process? How frequently do your teams engage in this?

- How do you approach digital attribution for all environments (display/in-app/video/search/CTV)?

- How do you connect digital attribution workstreams to attribution also concerned with broader investments?

- How do you de-pollute any campaign analytics and/or re-targeting efforts from IVT?

Part of the issue is posing the right kinds of questions externally, but this has to be backed up with some internal inquiries. It's equally important, in order for transparency checks to be fully made, to be able to raise the right kinds of questions internally.

Transparency workstreams have to be governed and owned. And driven. Otherwise they will never be undertaken properly—there are too many vested interests at play for the demystification of digital buying to be a naturally occurring phenomenon. Make it a KPI, set process targets, connect it to bonuses where appropriate.

"It is difficult to get [someone] to understand something when [their] salary depends upon [their] not understanding it" (Upton Sinclair, 1935).

Table 3.1 shows a framework that can facilitate this, which will enable an organizational self-diagnosis expressed in terms of *what tasks vs. what teams*. It will foster ownership of specific elements required for transparency workstreams. What tasks are the responsibility of what teams?

These functions represent a very diverse set of required skillsets. Not all skillsets and training requirements are appropriate for you. It is important to flush out any false sense of capabilities combined with an inherent digital skills gap, as this can result in widespread imposter syndrome.

But the talent game is not one that the ad industry has been winning in recent years.

Casting a wider recruitment net

On the client side, there is growing evidence that the industry is struggling to attract and retain appropriate talent.

A longitudinal study undertaken by the Chartered Institute of Marketing (CIM, 2022) in the UK observed and identified declining proficiencies in key disciplines: analytics and data, content marketing, digital strategy, e-commerce, online advertising, mobile marketing, social media, SEO, usability, and a handful more.

The test conducted by the CIM asked 7,000 participants to complete a series of tasks aimed at testing their knowledge in 12 disciplines of marketing, with a particular focus on digital skills, and calculated a percentage score for each.

Analytics and data skillsets have fallen the most, with almost seven in ten marketers (67 percent) falling into the lowest two quintiles for their analytics and data abilities. Whilst this might be "easy to explain," as new analytics options and changes in cookie rules raise the overall complexity of digital marketing, it is nonetheless a "worrying" indication of marketers' ability to analyze and improve their capabilities through hiring, training and retaining of key types of skillsets that are increasingly required.

Table 3.1 A sample grid for transparent workstreams

Team tasks	Central media management	Local media management	In-house media team	Media agency	Trading desk or tech partner	Auditor	Specialist
OPERATIONAL							
Partner selection							
Audience criteria							
KPI setting							
MEASUREMENT							
IVT measurement							
Viewability measurement							
Brand safety enforcement							
IMPLEMENTATION							
Ad tech implementation management							

(continued)

Table 3.1 (Continued)

Team tasks	Central media management	Local media management	In-house media team	Media agency	Trading desk or tech partner	Auditor	Specialist
Buying targets/saving validation							
Digital/programmatic trading							
INSIGHT & ANALYTICS							
Data science							
Data engineering							
Analysis & reporting							

On the plus side, senior members of marketing management teams were observed to be improving in terms of digital skills literacies, our own first-hand experience reflecting the same. A good thing for the future.

But it does still point to a recruitment malaise in advertising and marketing. In certain markets it has been associated with a limited recruitment pool—it is no secret that diversity, equity and inclusiveness (DEI) are a challenge for what has been a traditional career option for white middle-class males.

Functionally, the industry has to start casting a wider net. Not only in DEI terms, but also towards the core STEM skills that the industry, particularly on the agency and client side, so demands. The extent to which it can do so and compete with the rise of technology-driven start-ups remains to be seen.

There is a wide breadth of skills that advertising has always attracted. But let's be frank, it has not always been an equal opportunity zone.

On one side of the Atlantic the agency business was once associated with "toffs" who didn't want to be bankers, wannabe creative film makers, and middle-class chaps who thought media buying might be a more accessible form of city trading. The Wolverines of Wardour Street. On the other side of the Atlantic we had, well, Mad Men. And that's the point. Most were male. And white, and largely privileged.

In many ways this is an issue that persists to this day. The ad industry, like many others, has become good at making DEI pledges. It is beginning to get better at taking action and forming taskforces (4As, 2022). And it even now produces guidelines for media planners and buyers on how to ensure diversity and representation in audience planning and measurement (WFA, 2022).

Of course, not all forms of diversity are immediately visible to the naked eye, but you only have to spend an afternoon in an agency, or at a client's office, to recognize there is still a lot of work to be done. Overall, representation is getting better (15 percent of staff at media agencies and 12 percent of staff at creative and other agencies come from BAME backgrounds in the UK) and getting closer to societal demographic make-up (IPA, 2020). And diversity in agencies is growing year by year (IPA, 2021).

But there are multiple issues. Nearly half of all people in the UK, for example, consider themselves "working class" but the creative and media industries only have 23 percent of those who self-identify as such (Gov.uk, 2021). Elocution lessons are known to have been offered to those with different accents.

And there are challenges in terms of diverse representation at a C-suite level, where it is only just above 5 percent for those from a BAME background, which is well below targets. The industry is still run, for the most part, by old white guys.

We can let time run its course to develop the next generation of leaders from the current talent pool, or we can equate diversity with better overall skillsets, as we should, and support and accelerate these trends:

> When it comes down to it, it boils down to types of privilege and class. But the issues overlap. Class, gender, race, sexuality, disability, age… We make a point of working with and looking for the future of the industry, which is most definitely based on diversity of background and thinking. (Bakhtiari, 2022)

If, for a nanosecond, we put aside the moral imperative of doing so, the business case for diversity is clear. Companies with the best levels of diversity are 35 percent more likely to see financial results that exceed their country's average (McKinsey, 2015). Companies with more diverse teams are more likely to solve problems faster (Reynolds and Lewis, 2017). And greater levels of diversity can reduce the one thing that is the scourge of all talent pools—high turnover rates (Deloitte, 2018).

"Move aside, Gandalf"

Recruiting diverse talent at point of entry is key. But "at the other end" the industry also has to be careful to avoid complaints of ageism.

Most ad budgets tend to avoid targeting people over 50, which could seem strange given they have most of the wealth. There are of course multiple reasons why this happens and why brands have always deified and revered youthful consumers, with their promise of loyalty and "lifetime value."

The average age of staff in the largest agency holding companies remains under 30. Mark Read, the CEO of the largest one, WPP, had to apologize when he referred to this fact, particularly after adding, "they don't hark back to the 1980s, luckily" (Read, 2020).

Given that he was responding to a question on an investor call at the time, and specifically talking about getting "the balance right" between, e.g. traditional and digital skillsets, you can see the fine line being tread. It is of course wrong to assume that anyone over 30 is crap at digital. New thinking and fresh ideas can come from anywhere. By the same measure, the expertise (and earning power) that has traditionally come with age has a different shelf-life in a digital age driven by ever-changing tech platforms.

Staffing agencies and ad departments with young, cheap talent, and over-working them is not a sustainable business model.

People have always been the bedrock of the industry. Good clients will immediately recognize key team members who are the source of dispropor-tionate chunks of delivered service value. And for all of the technological revolution that has happened to the industry in the past few years, agencies remain stubbornly connected to FTE (full-time equivalent) people-based costings when submitting proposals at pitch. People provide margins.

2020 saw the steepest downturn in the industry's history with mass re-dundancies. There has been a bounce back since, but the advertising indus-try, like many others, has suffered as a result of the talent pool reassessing their employment and life-choice priorities.

There are many issues that have accelerated this for the industry. Yes, low pay might be cited as one, and the rise of the tech giants as employers and lack of inclusion all pre-date the pandemic.

If you are a new software engineering graduate entering the marketplace, where are you going to go if asked, Apple Inc or adland? The industry is also failing to attract and retain the right kind of talent. If you are a STEM graduate, your first thought might not be, "I fancy working in agency land."

The right teams, with the best technology, aligned with the right tasks

Putting together a cross-functional team is critical. One that can draw upon available technology aligned with each task at hand.

Below is a checklist of the teams and techniques required to improve transparency via the use of available metrics for you and your agency. The first set of priorities relate to determining the ease with which an independ-ent digital activity audit could be completed with a view to operationally bridging any measurement "Deltas."

There are a number of things you could refer to as "operational pre-requisites":

- **Brand intent:** Is there a desire within your company to begin to unpack the digital supply path and the resources available to manage a workstream?

- **Agency intent:** Do you have an agency partner that is open to engaging in such a workstream and can it be managed without impacting working relationships? Do they have similar intent and incentives?

- **Data and tech enablers:** Do we have access to the right kind of data that can facilitate transparent supply path analysis? Do we need an independent tech supplier?

- **Contractual enablers:** Do our contracts with our agencies and their intermediaries in the supply chain facilitate data sharing and access?

- **Third-party operational intent:** Do those intermediaries in the supply chain have incentives or open intent to participate?

- **Legal compliance on data shares:** Are the techniques we are going to use future-proofed in the sense that they are not cookie-dependent and/or do not involve the use of any personal identifiers?

There are then a number of things you could refer to as "pipeline prerequisites":

- **Persistent means of measuring impressions:** Can our measurement technique be operationalized and scaled over time? Or is this going to be a one-off deep dive?

- **Persistent means of measuring quality:** Do we have ad verification partners in place, with technology that can facilitate getting a read on 100 percent of digital events?

- **Persistent third-party data access:** Will our third-party trading partners offer persistent data shares, and can we get access to a regular data feed?

There are also a number of things you could refer to as "operational barriers":

- **Ability to deploy tech:** Do the media types and formats that we buy lend themselves to measurement? Where is our technology-based transparency measurement feasible and where is it not? (For example, are all of our bought environments friendly for JavaScript-based methods or only image pixel types of methods)?

- **Ability to extract DSP logs that measure bids won:** Will our DSP partners provide regular data feeds? And do we have the data-handling and extraction capabilities?

- **Means of integrating verification data:** Can we combine those DSP logs with our data from our verification partners? (Is there enough granularity on both sides to enable a matching)?

- **Ability to map verification data with exchange propensities:** Can we parse out the results by exchange to determine the propensity of each exchange to deliver quality traffic?

- **Ability to map verification data with traffic source propensities:** Can we parse out the results by source to determine the propensity of each traffic source to deliver quality traffic?

- **Assessment of DSP/site partner propensities:** Can we parse out the results by buying partner to determine the propensity of each traffic-buying partner to deliver quality traffic?

The last set of tasks relate to making sure that all of the insights you have gained into the quality of your digital supply can be acted upon. Your teams (be they internal or agency-based) will have to be able to analyze the data from available tech with a view to improving measurement and supply path optimization. It's a good thing to check that your agency is doing this now anyway:

- Are ad-server measures being used regularly (impression ID, placement ID, quality metrics)?

- Is there ongoing persistent matching of datasets and analytics (discrepancies, supply sources × quality metrics)?

- Are your agency or team regularly accessing DSP logs (bid ID, source URL, exchange ID)?

It's equally important to create space for "getting it wrong."

Leaders who know how to avoid mistakes, especially serious ones, are far more valuable in digital advertising than those who chase industry awards. The exacerbation of quality issues in digital is rooted in a lack of understanding of landscape mechanics. It is those mechanics, and not malicious intent, that are the source of most transparency and measurement challenges.

"Optimizing" a product or a process involves initially *identifying the bad, not immediately replicating the good*. And this by definition is often best done in retrospect and with clarity, honesty, and openness. To outsource anything properly you have to have at least *some* of the skills to recognize good from bad.

Everyone sees success stories reported in digital advertising. Rarely do companies disclose their failures. As such, it shouldn't be surprising that many leaders in large and mid-size organizations have not truly taken ownership of their efforts.

Many advertisers and media directors feel like there's a *secret sauce* to buying digital media efficiently and most agency sales pitches suggest that as the case. But that is part of the sales pitch as an agent of any kind—the notion that someone is paid to understand the rules and get results so someone else doesn't have to do it.

Unfortunately, this skills gap is equally prevalent in the world of media agencies and even digital-focused shops, where recruitment has not been focused nearly enough on technical roles, nor bringing systems experts to the forefront of decision making. The first step in closing the gap is to identify the functions needed to successfully plan, manage, and execute digital advertising campaigns.

Digital advertising is not simply a media exercise, it is now a practice of problem solving in the realms of internet architecture navigation, content consumption analysis, big data, software procurement, complex systems intervention, and behavioral economics. Staff accordingly, and rope in independent experts where necessary, to foster a culture of "fail fast, but learn."

References

4As (2022) Now. New. Next. Talent and the future of work, https://www.aaaa.org/now-new-next-talent-and-the-future-of-work/?cn-reloaded=1 (archived at https://perma.cc/V94F-ZAMQ)

Adgate, B (2021) The fastest growing video advertising platform is now CTV, *Forbes*, https://www.forbes.com/sites/bradadgate/2021/10/13/the-fastest-growing-video-advertising-platform-is-now-ctv/?sh=494fdddaf833 (archived at https://perma.cc/H6DA-KYS9)

Bakhtiari, K (2022) Authors' interview with Kian Bakhtiari, Founder of The People.Work, a creative consultancy for a more inclusive and sustainable future

Blodwell, W (2022) Authors' interview with Wayne Blodwell of The Programmatic Advisory

CIM (2022) Marketers' Digital Skills Survey, https://www.cim.co.uk/newsroom/research-digital-skills-in-decline-during-pandemic/ (archived at https://perma.cc/FVP3-GUTJ)

Deloitte (2018) Unleashing the power of inclusion, https://www2.deloitte.com/content/dam/Deloitte/us/Documents/about-deloitte/us-about-deloitte-unleashing-power-of-inclusion.pdf (archived at https://perma.cc/EWG6-KUDW)

eMarketer (2022) CTV and digital advertising: How Connected TV is one of the fastest growing channels in 2022, https://www.insiderintelligence.com/insights/ctv-fastest-growing-channel-digital-advertising/ (archived at https://perma.cc/39YU-4DNE)

Foster, S (2021) WFA survey shows clients all at sea as they try to navigate digital media, *More About Advertising*, https://www.moreaboutadvertising.com/2021/09/wfa-survey-shows-clients-all-at-sea-as-they-try-to-navigate-digital-media/ (archived at https://perma.cc/7N3F-NG55)

Gov.uk (2021) Social Mobility Barometer, 2021, https://www.gov.uk/government/publications/social-mobility-barometer-2021/social-mobility-barometer-public-attitudes-to-social-mobility-in-the-uk (archived at https://perma.cc/5TPF-PSH4)

IAB (2018) Internet Advertising Bureau, Transparency and Consent Framework https://iabeurope.eu/transparency-consent-framework/ (archived at https://perma.cc/RYV2-787S)

IPA (2020) IPA Agency Census 2020, https://ipa.co.uk/knowledge/publications-reports/agency-census-2020 (archived at https://perma.cc/UL4U-X2PU)

IPA (2021) IPA Agency Census 2021, https://ipa.co.uk/knowledge/publications-reports/agency-census-2021/ (archived at https://perma.cc/Q2UB-86KG)

Lomas, N (2022) Adtech's compliance theatre is headed to Europe's top court. It's privacy crunch time for 'consent' to track, *Techcrunch*, https://techcrunch.com/2022/09/07/iab-europe-tcf-gdpr-breach-appeal/ (archived at https://perma.cc/PJ6S-EJPP)

McKinsey (2015) Why Diversity Matters, https://www.mckinsey.com/capabilities/people-and-organizational-performance/our-insights/why-diversity-matters (archived at https://perma.cc/3QM2-D3GG)

Read, M (2020) Mark Read, WPP CEO, on an investor call August 2020, *Marketing Week*, https://www.marketingweek.com/mark-read-age-remarks-problem/ (archived at https://perma.cc/2V7X-JMWS)

Reynolds, A and Lewis, D (2017) Teams Solve Problems Faster When They're More Cognitively Diverse, *Harvard Business Review*, https://hbr.org/2017/03/teams-solve-problems-faster-when-theyre-more-cognitively-diverse (archived at https://perma.cc/H32R-JPJM)

Sinclair, U (1935) *I, Candidate for Governor*, Farrar & Reinhart Inc

TRU (2022) The 2022 Data Privacy Jobs Report by TRU Staffing Partners https://info.trustaffingpartners.com/2022-data-privacy-jobs-report (archived at https://perma.cc/VE5A-49JT)

WFA (2021) The Media Capability Gap, https://wfanet.org/knowledge/item/2021/08/02/The-Media-Capability-Gap (archived at https://perma.cc/G6AK-P62K)

WFA (2022) Guide to Diversity in Media Planning and Buying, https://wfanet.org/knowledge/item/2022/01/21/WFA-launches-guide-to-diversity-and-representation-in-media-planning-and-buying (archived at https://perma.cc/8SW6-AG9D)

When and how   04
to consult
external
partners

As outlined in the previous chapter, there are some clear challenges for advertisers when it comes to approaching the digital ecosystem. Challenges that are as much about developing skillsets as they are about managing finite resources and existing capabilities.

Some advertisers look for help, and some do not. For every marketer who cries for outside intervention and support, there is another who ponders if they should be doing all of this on their own. Which always makes people question, "what bits of it?", "who have we got that can do that?" and "how?"

The answers to those questions and the degree to which brands are reliant on external agency groups are evolving. New types of potential partners also have new roles to take on. The World Federation of Advertisers (WFA) claim that 80 percent of advertisers now use in-house marketing services of one sort or another, and that 75 percent are only "somewhat satisfied" or less with their current agency (WFA, 2022).

Relationships are clearly strained, but is taking things in-house the answer?

In 2016, Unilever launched a network of in-house content production studios to operate across its offices worldwide, aimed at producing cheaper, faster, and better content. In 2019, TSB launched its own in-house content studio to revive its marketing team, deliver content at speed, and cut down on agency costs.

The drivers of in-housing can be numerous. To tackle this, you need to understand what you're looking for. Are you hoping for better control? Increased savings or efficiencies? Increased transparency? Faster execution? Specific efficiencies for different functions?

In order to understand the nuanced dynamics of if, when and how to do something "in-house," every marketing budget owner should remember how we collectively got here and make it clear where they want to go.

Proxies of the past and present

The very beginnings of agencies involved the outsourcing of some functions.

The question of outsourcing was less about advertisers "ceding any control," and more about some opportunistic traders who saw and created a new marketplace.

Back in 1842, one such trader, named Volney B. Palmer, quite famously bought media space in bulk at various newspapers and then resold the space at higher rates to advertisers. The actual creative ad unit was prepared in-house by the client themselves, which basically made Palmer little more than an ad-space broker, albeit inventing an industry while he was at it.

One could argue that he was nothing more than a sales agent for the publishing side. He might have agreed, describing his company as "the duly authorized agent of most of the best newspapers" (Holland, 1974).

He was transparent and aware about who he was representing and where his incentives leaned. Hence the first organized use of the phrase "agency" in advertising had little to do with representing advertiser interests, and more to do with opportunistically brokering for the "sell side."

Many other advertising agencies soon followed the same business model until a new form of agency, rather than simply selling space, provided a full range of services, including planning, creating, and executing complete campaigns for its customers.

You won't find too many brand owners today who are interested in this kind of Palmer-esque setup. Today, most advertisers demand that agencies represent their interests and not those of the media owners. And if there is anything most companies now want to keep in-house, it is more focused on media than it is creative or content production functions.

Creative workstreams, by definition, are hard to process and package concisely. Impactful work is often difficult to replicate at will. It's easy to demonstrate that in-housing creativity, more often than not, doesn't produce great work. Pepsi's in-house-created Kendall Jenner ad in 2017 is one the industry is still trying to forget. But they tend to be the high-profile, long-form, big-idea, types of creatives that just don't seem to sit well with client-based production teams. When it comes to what you could refer to as "low-level, high-frequency" creative asset production, it's a different story. Basically, everything from a tweet all the way through to social outreach, and building cheap and cheerful assets for performance marketing. That tends to sit better with client-side production teams.

Media buying is a different fish. It's now all about data and measurement, the lifeblood of budgetary control and media decision making. And if you are a client with large first-party data assets, it is wise from both a business and compliance perspective to take control of activating that data.

So, running the risk of oversimplifying how you should initially classify your business as being in-house friendly or not, consider Table 4.1.

Platforms pulling strings

There are now a plethora of digital technology providers, all of which are offering their technology directly to whoever wants to use it. And they are agnostic as to who should use it.

As a result, the in-housing of the access, oversight, and operation of media buying and measurement technology is one of the first things that they ponder. Google doesn't care if it's you, an advertiser, or your agency who have fingers on keyboards when it comes to using, DV360, for example.

This has caused a wave of hushed disintermediation across traditional media agency groups. Technology platforms offering new direct relationships. Self-serve tools making it easier to buy direct from media platforms.

The act of buying media space has never been so democratized in its accessibility. Bulk negotiation leverage and periodic joint industry measurement

Table 4.1   To in-house or not to in-house?

	First-party data rich	Not data rich
High frequency "low level" performance-focused ads	Strongly consider in-housing as an option to protect and leverage own data	Be careful. You might just end up using other people's data and tech (just replicating agencies)
Low frequency, less performance-focused ads	Consider it an option but it will be a challenge to connect your workstreams with your data	Don't bother even thinking about in-housing

have both been replaced with technology-enabled decision making and granular live measurement at scale. DSP tech players allow brands to run online advertising campaigns with precise targeting and collect large amounts of user data. Some have seen higher return on investment and lower costs.

In effect, brands today can increasingly afford to almost bypass the ad agency and head straight to AdTech companies instead. If an advertiser wants "hands on keyboards," it's up to any in-house team to use the data, but far more importantly it's also up to them to carry out whatever validation they believe to be necessary. Which in and of itself requires another relationship with third-party verification specialists. Another set of geeks. Another set of technology, which is neither yours nor your agency's.

With the advent of the digital era, AdTech companies started disrupting and threatening the way ad agencies operated. They shifted the balance of power away from agencies. Agencies do have the platform usage skills, but what they're too often missing is the incentive to use them in an in-depth and productive manner.

It is common for platforms to strike agreements with agencies and give those agencies KPIs and targets to sell to their client base. In many ways, an agency representing bulk inventory in 1841 has been replaced in the 21st century with an agency being glorified resellers of other people's ad technology.

To remain competitive, agencies do often operate custom, in-house AdTech solutions. They do themselves of course outsource some of the work to trading desk partners. There are a number of successful companies in the programmatic space, for example, who build up available technologies with their own data science approaches or buying algorithms. They tend to be an additional layer between your agency and even DSPs on occasion. But they do add value, particularly when your buying agency is under-skilled in a specific area or overworked.

All of which begs the question, if you have a contract with a media agency inside one of the holding groups, but they in turn outsource some programmatic buying functions to a third-party trading desk with extra data science capability, and they in turn use the DSPs that everyone would be using anyway.... (1) what's the value add in that chain... and (2) who exactly is your agency?

More often than not, though, your buying agency does have hands on keyboards, but they use the same technology and datasets available to everyone.

This offers an impetus for brands and their management to own the required tech relationships directly, and increasingly leads to many media budget controllers being asked by their CMOs when they will be in-housing their media operations.

It also begs the question of whether full diligence is undertaken when contracting with your agency in the first place.

How to outsource

There are therefore a number of pitfalls associated with inappropriate housing. Just as there are a plethora of traps associated with inappropriate use of external help.

As any friendly lawyer will tell you, the basis of a good, healthy, trusting partner relationship is a contract. In order to secure transparency and trust, the WFA, in their 2022 Media Contract Guidance update to members, recommend any contract cover the following 10 critical areas (WFA/Firm Decisions, 2022):

1 The Master Service Agreement (MSA)

2 The challenges of digital media

3 Transparent models in programmatic media buying

4 Inventory media

5 Unbilled media, media credits and holds

6 Media benefits, including agency volume benefits (AVBs)

7 The right to audit

8 Data management

9 Payment terms

10 Remuneration

Around half of the top global advertisers revisit and audit their contract regularly (at least once per year). This leaves about half of the industry in the camp of those who do not, which is a bit of a showstopper for anyone keeping an eye out for transparency.

Contract compliance and financial audits are not new to the industry. What is relatively new, though, is an array of broader issues that demand diligence with external partners.

The contract, while unable to account for every nuance, is the appropriate place to enshrine all these additional material criteria:

- Do your partners ensure that your brand appears in contexts that are safe?

- Do your partners ensure the protection of your first-party data and any private information?

- Do your partners ensure that disinformation is not funded?

- Do your partners ensure that your media is being bought in accordance with your company's DEI goals?

- Do your partners offer a responsible media supply chain that is built for the future and serves the needs of everyone, especially consumers?

You don't have to conduct a full-blown investigation to see how safety controls have gone awry in the digital advertising space. It is also not difficult to see the general lack of guardrails—ones that need to exist to help brands avoid being ripped off or taken advantage of.

Agency management guidelines

For any master service agreement (MSA) between an advertiser and an agency, there are a number of fundamentals that have to be in place from the advertiser's perspective.

For example, companies need a dedicated SOW (scope of work) that outlines the tasks and deliverables associated with the agency assignment. This should itemize:

- team members, responsibilities and time spent on your business;

- agency tools utilized, if at all, and for what tasks;

- a service-level agreement (SLA) for specific and overall deliverables;

- specific agreed cadences for reporting and optimizations towards agreed KPIs.

Companies also need a clear sense of commercial rates and rebates associated with agency "inventory partners." For example, agencies may strike individual direct deals with publishers but still fulfill them programmatically.

Make sure you have contractual references to varying rights to data, and access to platforms used by the agency and any other partners. This can include audit access rights but will vary depending on each MSA.

There is clearly a resilience about agency holding groups.

In an attempt to keep up with Big Tech, the likes of WPP have funneled huge amounts of money into digital transformation in recent years. This has borne some fruit—WPP's digital advertising revenues have recently surged by 32 percent and digital advertising on pure-play platforms now represents over two-thirds of the group's total advertising sales.

They are not alone, as others such as Publicis, Dentsu, and Omnicom have all strived to redefine their digital and data chops in the last few years. They are beginning to make hay where the sun currently shines—in digital performance marketing, e-commerce, and diversifying from the old model to a wider range of services across a much broader spectrum, going beyond the old ad model into new content creation and channel- and platform-based expertise/services. Like super-tankers making a slow turn given some headwinds that started a decade or more ago. Younger upstarts like S4C, at least initially, have benefitted from a programmatic, digital and data focus from the get-go. If a great contract is the basis of trust and transparency, then getting some visibility on who else might be involved, beyond the agency, is a must.

When working with these kinds of partners, a brand's management has to be intensely observant and also regularly involved. Agency groups work with a plethora of outside partners, and you may just be sacrificing your own control for a hidden third party. If a good agency–client relationship is like a good marriage, then you will want to know what the in-laws are like.

Knowing who you are working with, and in turn who they work with, and what you are paying for, is foundational for the management of agency–client relationships and avoiding the principal-agent problem.

There have been many reported instances where the services an advertiser thinks they are buying from an agency differ from what they receive. For example, it is often the case that your agency may be farming out some of the contracted services you have agreed for them to undertake. And they may or may not have disclosed this. There have been more than a few examples of when a third party has been subcontracted by an agency to undertake programmatic buying for a specific client, and the client is totally unaware.

In other instances, the agency may or may not have disclosed additional hidden interests when it comes to recommending one platform over another. It is common for agencies to be contracted as resellers of other people's technology—and separate, undisclosed agreements and KPIs for agencies from Google or other tech platform providers may already be in place.

It is important, therefore, to ask your agency how they will manage the requisite buy-side technology associated with your business:

- Which tech partners are being used?
- What separate agreements are in place with them that impact agency recommendations?
- Are there any third parties being activated in a managed service manner?
- If so, what fees are involved?
- Who owns the contract with the buying technology provider?
  - o Does that contract offer data access?
- Will there be any additional data providers?

Independence is a virtue

It's always a good thing to have an independent voice to call upon in any relationship. As such, media auditors and verification specialists can regularly be called upon and should be contractually involved. At best they can act like independent and skilled arbiters of an agreed truth—like a welcome marriage counselor who gives guidance based on a deep understanding of the nature of the characters and tasks at hand. At worst, they can act like unskilled destructive forces who do not always have digital buying literacy nor the appropriate technology to audit at scale.

The verification partner brings the technology and scale of data required to fulfill digital audits, whilst the auditor tends to bring a holistic view of all spends and strategic auditing frameworks. All of which should lead to a better assessment of the quality of inventory being bought by the agency (to contextualize reported costs).

What is often required is some guidance on how an advertiser can manage these quality assessment partners:

- What media formats are covered by the verification tech provider and how (display, video, CTV etc.)?
- At what scale (is 100 percent coverage of measurable environments offered)?
- What environments are unmeasurable (e.g. the limits of JavaScript technology or the specific methods deployed by the partner in question)?

- How much coverage is offered of the walled-garden environments and how will it be provided?
- Are measures provided for IVT, viewability, brand safety, and in-geo?
- Are they an accredited supplier (e.g. MRC)?
- At what point in the supply chain are they measuring (e.g. is it a pre-bid or post-bid measure? Is the measure taken at the bid stream or client side?)
- How do they specifically count impressions?

Until recently, many auditors have been criticized for having defunct techniques for the digital age, and an overall lack of digital literacy. This is changing and, if deployed, it is best to deploy both an auditor and a verification partner in unison.

As outlined in a previous chapter, auditors have always been obsessed with "cost versus quality" assessments in media buying: "Was the media buy in line with targeted quality parameters, and was the cost competitive?"

In order to answer the "quality" part of the above question, auditors must now be deployed in conjunction with verification specialists or another provider of granular datasets that cover things like IVT/viewability/brand safety/in-geo quality scores. For every ad event where possible.

In order to answer the "cost" part of the above question, it now involves the use of log-level data from available buying platforms.

As a result, some auditors have reverted to focusing on the "contract compliance" of the "pitch consultancy space," but the good ones know also how to use technology and available datasets to approach the remit of original media auditors. Given the increasing number of different organizations involved in the planning and buying supply chain, all with their own commercial interests, it could be argued that simple contract compliance audits have become even more important. It can be useful to run data/impression count audits and the money supply/contractual compliance audits in unison, but the skillsets involved are usually different.

Take back control, only if you really want to

A massive percentage of total ad spend now goes to media formats and companies whose principles of measurement are untouched by any form of independent evaluation or audit, but whose tools and systems can, if needed, form the basis of in-house trading. A bit like Brexiteers, many in adland have been seduced by notions of "taking back control." Be that fully taking control of digital media buys, or some kind of managed service arrangement.

Some industry observers, especially those that value agency contributions, think that the control offered to in-house entities is illusory and dangerous. Tech behemoths often provide data that is not always verified nor is it necessarily verifiable because of a disparate taxonomy. And many advertisers have convinced themselves that the numbers given to them by those doing the selling are correct and valuable.

Other observers and digital transformation advocates would contend that agency disintermediation is a healthy thing, and that in the era of privacy concerns, it has never been more important to consider degrees of in-housing and control. Managing the media function has become increasingly complicated, and it is a moot point as to where the capability exists as long as a brand's media function is being managed.

And in many ways, it's not a zero-sum game, in that it can be more nuanced than simply "taking something back from agencies."

Either way, a means of assessing if, how, and when to bring something in-house is a prerequisite. Below is a baseline agenda for that first brainstorming session with key team members:

1 Understanding what your current media management process looks like:

   a. Map out your resource strengths and weaknesses

   b. Determine how easy it would be to scale each element

   c. Be aware of where your current contractual commitments are

2 Prioritize:

   a. Which areas will be the easiest/hardest to build (in operational terms)

   b. Which areas will be the easiest/hardest to build (in cost terms)

   c. Which are of most value in relation to your own goals

3 Develop an action road map (in terms of "Now" vs "Next" vs "Future").

Getting clear evidence of the value of your existing partnerships is good. Working with them in a transparent manner is great.

Even if you are still motivated and driven to own your own processes and paddle your own canoe, be aware that it can be an operational nightmare. There is an ongoing backlash against in-housing, which is driven at least partially by the fact that many have tried it who shouldn't have, and for those that should have and did, they did it wrong.

Here is a watch-out checklist:

Connect in-house capability to business goals and owned data: you need to have a clear set of reasons "why."

Don't do it just to save money: you cannot fall into the trap of treating any owned ad capability as simply a cost center.

Don't underestimate resource management: especially in the "performance" side of the digital ad industry, the number of partners and processes involved can be daunting.

Don't underestimate potential in-housing failure: success stories for in-housing are rarer than the trade press would have you believe.

Don't underestimate the complexities of media: the range of skillsets required to manage a complex media plan is a heady mixture. And an ever-evolving one.

Don't underestimate the complexities of the billing and reconciliation back end: we cannot stress enough how important this one is. The back-end reconciliation of finances in media trading will eat a lot of your resources if you are not careful.

When asked, in 2022, 150 CMOs were scathing of the challenges involved. Nearly half (43 percent) of all marketers think in-housing is an operational nightmare, while two-fifths (39 percent) say teams lack creative inspiration and a third (33 percent) reckon it is difficult to implement; 27 percent were unconvinced that it works, but most (80 percent) think it should be improved (Collective/Content, 2022).

The same survey cited that about 77 percent of CMOs were looking for a different model. They just haven't found one that suits them yet.

There is a strong case for advertisers to stop thinking about in-housing vs not in-housing, and start thinking about hybrid models.

Boots/Walgreens launched a new marketing agency, tapping into the retailer's loyalty club data to deliver personalized campaigns for brand owners. Dubbed Boots Media Group, the agency is a joint venture with the media agency Threefold and offers a full-service proposition that places the data of Boots Advantage Card's 17 million active members at the heart of the business.

A data-rich retailer launching an agency. This feels like a suitable hybrid experiment that takes advantage of an advertiser's great assets whilst trying to maintain a separate culture from the mothership. Those that underestimate "agency culture" underestimate the power of people retention. As the saying goes in adland, "culture eats strategy for lunch" in terms of productivity and minimizing churn of the one thing that ironically this era of advertising continues to rely on—good people.

Interestingly, this is also happening at a time when one of the emergent forces shaping the industry is the new retail media network appearing. Many of the large global retailers are now launching their own retail media networks, spying a lucrative future business model that offers a win-win for both brand and retailer, as we will see in a later chapter.

References

Collective Content Studio (2022) The in-house marketing model, reimagined, https://blog.collectiveworld.com/content-studio/ (archived at https://perma.cc/MWW3-S8X5)

Holland, D R (1974) Volney B. Palmer: The nation's first advertising agency man, *The Pennsylvania Magazine of History and Biography*, **98** (3) pp 353–81

WFA (2022) WFA Agency Roster Transformation Report in conjunction with Observatory International, https://wfanet.org/knowledge/item/2022/07/19/Agency-Roster-Transformation (archived at https://perma.cc/87LX-QAKS)

WFA/Firm Decisions (2022) Media Contract Guidance for Advertisers, https://wfanet.org/knowledge/item/2022/02/28/Media-Contract-Guidance-for-Advertisers-Global-Best-Practice (archived at https://perma.cc/97BC-E63F)

The limits of tech

05

In the previous chapter we began by mapping the different relationships that any manager of advertising now relies upon, with advertiser–agency relations often sitting at the epicenter of a myriad of other more technology-focused partnerships.

We have also outlined how a lot of these relationships can be considered "asymmetrical," with advertisers dealing with technology partners who have very different knowledge bases, as well as misaligned approaches to things like trading transparencies and data provision.

An advertiser of consumer goods may not have the required tech experience built into their CV to deal with these partners, nor the required tech DNA within their organization or company, especially if its core business is not technology-led. They need help, and that help can't always come from an agency partner who could be incentivized to be nothing more than a glorified seller of third-party technology, or whose incentives are more aligned with technology suppliers and less with their on-paper advertiser clients.

This dynamic can be seen in the way that publicly traded agency holding companies establish commercial arrangements with the ad platforms. The 2016 study conducted by the Association of National Advertisers and investigation firm K2 Intelligence, reported: "Numerous non-transparent business practices, including cash rebates to media agencies, were found to be pervasive in the U.S. media ad buying ecosystem." (K2, 2016).

What the investigators are referring to, in practice, is that if an agency can guarantee a media owner or seller $50 million in spend, the agency could be given a steep "consulting fee" at the end of the fiscal year in the range of $5–$8 million from the media owner or seller. All the while, the collective clients of the agency were charged $75 million in charges, inclusive of fees to "plan" and "execute" the advertising plan, while being kept in the dark about the biased relationship with the owner/seller of the media.

This may be "status quo" for some, but to an unbiased mind, this would seem like a principal-agent problem: a betrayal of the interests of the client. The truth as usual lies somewhere in between, because agency corporations able to engage in these practices must be at the largest scale. Publicly traded companies do have some baseline legal requirements of financial transparency and can be held to account, but only really by their shareholders and investor representatives. There is always less power lying with the customer or client of a large publicly traded company versus a small privately owned business. Active radical transparency cures many woes caused by the free market, including share prices impacted by bad press.

This is perfect territory for the flourishing of unchallenged false and exaggerated impacts associated with technologies that may or may not have teeth, promoted by armies of industry salespeople, funded by VC money, and taking advantage of advertisers operating in unfamiliar new terrains.

The truth, the whole truth, and anything but the truth

The marketing and advertising industry can fall victim to exaggerated claims in the same way that everyday consumers can fall victim to the promoted benefits of any product.

In consumer marketing, there is of course nothing wrong with great branded messaging like Wheaties' "Breakfast of Champions" or Nike's "Just Do It." It's only when it comes to the world of explicit product benefits that there can be sometimes incomplete evidence or questionable claims. When, e.g., a toothpaste brand says that nine out of 10 dentists would recommend theirs, they don't also disclose that those nine dentists also recommend most of the other 20 brands in the category. It is often simply a form of "nuanced" if incomplete messaging. And fair game.

In the world of marketing the ad technologies themselves, it's beyond nuanced. The gold rush associated with the growth of the sector has involved a deception on a completely different scale. It's called lying. At best, overselling.

How can advertisers deal with such vendors in this hyperbolic digital marketing world? It involves understanding that a lot of these promises ignore the reality and limits of technology as it currently exists. And advertisers need processes and skillsets that help them assess their suppliers accordingly.

The pitfalls of procedural procurement

A lot of companies have approaches to the procurement of technology that may not quite be fit for purpose. One of our favorite examples is from our own participation in dozens of request-for-proposal (RFP) processes conducted by the digital media and procurement teams of large Fortune 500 companies.

More than half the time, it was evident from the first day that the wonderful people we got to work with were simply following an instruction manual prepared for them by their agency of record, or a team from a big consulting firm that had flown in the previous month and expensed all their $50 lunches while reading "WTF is [insert topic in question]" articles on Digiday for "research."

The rest were more thoughtful, inquisitive, and sincere.

As verification technology and measurement software providers, for us the most inflammatory feature requirement in the cookie-cutter documents was always "pre-bid viewability." Even the thoughtful and inquisitive folks hadn't stopped to think about why anyone would ever buy non-viewable ad space if given the choice. But at one unfortunate moment in years past, the salesperson from a first-generation verification company convinced an underinformed media lead at a big agency that his "tech team" had created an algorithm that was able to prevent their budget from being spent on non-viewable ad placements in their real-time bidding for the low price of $0.25 CPM (cost per thousand).

A media buyer who has seen years of headlines and industry studies that say "Only half of digital ads are viewable" can see this as a golden exclusive opportunity to spend less than 10 percent of his current spend to ensure 100 percent of the ads are viewable. Math done at a cocktail-abundant lunch can suggest that's 40 percent ROI and you can verbally commit to implementing across 50 clients and 10 billion impressions per month!

In reality the feature called "pre-bid viewability" is simply a threshold set by a buyer, let's say 80 percent, that becomes a buy-side requirement in the bid request from a supply-side server, to include the measured historical viewable rate of impressions of that specific publisher ID.

So, there is no guarantee that the ad will be 80 percent viewable, or at all, only that the specific placement (i.e. the 300×250 banner ad in the login page of a sports betting app) has been measured as "*viewable*" (50 percent of the pixels or more) at least 80 percent of the times since it was initially created by the app owner. You can see that we are now a hop, skip and a jump from the dock with nothing but water under our feet.

It's technology, Jim, as we currently know it

There are natural limits to most things, most often imposed by the environment in which they operate. Technology is no different, the internet too. Internet technologies don't exist in vacuums or silos. The intertwined nature of the mechanics of the web is right there in the word *inter*net itself. An intertwined network of computing machines that store and deliver information upon request. They live and operate in the environments for which they were created and are subject to the rules and limitations imposed by those environments.

The internet as we know it today was at least 40 years in the making. And according to one of the founders of the very first network of machines (ARPANET) it wasn't originally about communication at all, but simply a means for scientists to share computing power simultaneously. The physical principles remain the same today: (i) a network of devices, plus (ii) a networking infrastructure that enables those devices to communicate, supported by (iii) efficient ways of avoiding congestion in busy networks. With scale came the need to make communications between devices easier, which gave birth to myriad cottage industry efforts. A patchwork quilt of technology if ever there was one.

The limits or constraints of the capabilities of the connected network system come both from hardware and physical limitations, and software and design limitations. It's important, as a marketer, to know whether you're driving on the information highway in a two-door Mini Cooper or a four-door GMC Sierra pick-up truck in order to gauge your operational exposure to various issues and what tools you have at your disposal to stay on track. Extreme weather elements, like traffic patterns, can slow down the Mini but not the GMC truck; but the truck requires a commitment of fuel resources as a higher baseline cost.

The number of devices is growing exponentially with the number of smartphones, tablets, and other network-connected gadgets now far outnumbering humans on the planet. The number of connected devices worldwide is forecast to almost triple from 9.7 billion in 2020 to more than 29 billion in 2030 (Statista, 2022a). But there is an ongoing worldwide shortage of the chips that drive them. And they represent an increasingly finite resource, with many being stockpiled as a result.

Networking infrastructure, and avoiding traffic congestion, remain bottlenecked challenges (a phenomenon known as "bufferbloat"). Our digital lives are all limited by the capacity of available physical processing infrastructure in the cables or routers that distribute it, or the data packeting efficiencies that underpin it. For all the apparent unbridled infinity of the internet, there are some real physical constraints around the hardware that currently underpins it.

However, whilst the hardware landscape of the internet can have natural limits, we are not wrong in thinking of the content ecosystem of the internet as totally infinite.

As things stand, there are an estimated 1.1 billion websites on the internet today, with thousands more being created every day (Siteefy, 2022). A long-tail phenomenon if ever there was one, with infinite niche opportunities.

Whatever your area of interest as a consumer of content and information, there is something out there for you. And for your brand, there are segments of audiences of every demographic and affinity combination. The only limitation is our imagination, as the saying goes. And of course, the ability to measure the advertising activity at scale.

That imagination shouldn't extend to believing that digital traffic, or human eyeballs on your campaigns, is infinite, though. This is not always easy or necessary when pursuing targets of outcomes or KPIs that are agnostic to the details of the reporting process (think pre-bid viewability targeting). Each individual instance where a marketer, even unwittingly, shortcuts their way to favorable KPIs can seem benign, but no snowflake in an avalanche ever feels responsible.

The long tail of content can only properly serve advertisers if there is complete and radical transparency. Without that, it results in an imbalance of power away from the advertiser and towards publishers. With a lot of the long tail of content, often many separate content owners can be bundled up under one publisher entity and only declare the presence of that public face.

This started with the practice of "audience extension" but is also evident with cases like Tumblr's attempt at winning back advertiser favor by banning adult content in 2018 after a press expose showed that thousands of pornography pages were being monetized with ads and being sold to advertisers as simply "Tumblr.com" in the reporting.

Digital ad supply not only needs better labeling, but buyers of ads must also read labels fully and be wary of packages with limited information. When we buy honey or bread at a farmer's market, we don't have uneasiness in packaging without a nutrition label because we are face to face with the producer. Few of us would buy a bottle of honey at a national supermarket that simply said "Honey" without explicit trust in the retailer. Again, the intangible nature of the goods being sold is as fleeting as the impact of their low quality. "Trust but verify" is a common phrase recycled at advertising conferences over the past decade, but it's critical for marketers to know how to verify before making their purchase.

Suppliers of "unlimited advertising opportunities"

Calculating the "average number of ads that an average consumer sees today" is sometimes like playing virtual bingo with all possible numbers in all languages: everyone has a different number, and it's a very dramatic difference at that.

"The average person sees 4,000–10,000 ads per day" says the source-less axiom that has made confident appearances in hundreds of articles and presentations. That's a very busy average person, in a very cluttered average day, who must be seeing around 10 ads per minute if we don't count the ones they see in their sleep (which the industry hasn't found a way to charge for, quite yet).

Equally ridiculous are the estimated number of available digital impressions at any given time. If you were to add up the "ad opportunities" provided by all of the current vendors of digital traffic, it would surpass 50 times the current population of the planet (including those without any internet connection).

These numbers clearly often lack a totally independent arbiter, and in this environment, it's easy to be a seller of ad opportunities.

It's a vendor paradise.

Checking the number of tech vendors in play in adland at any given time is exhausting. According to the ANA, just 10 years ago there were 350. Today, there are close to 10,000. Ironically, that's the same number of ads that one "average person" sees daily. Are we to imagine a live scenario where there are 10,000 pieces of technology out there all delivering 10,000 ads to one average person in one typical day?

Brands and media agencies often hear of these new technology offerings from conferences or trade group events and presentations. These are mostly "pay-to-play" events. Whilst that model of exposure to new technology is not unique to this industry, it can have the effect of fostering an unnatural bias towards shiny new suppliers that are supported by venture capital monies, with bold claims of solving age-old problems with things like machine learning, artificial intelligence, or other buzzwords that sit well in a funding deck.

It's not possible that all these vendors can have a unique way to make your digital advertising *more* efficient or effective, but it doesn't stop them claiming as much. There is clear evidence of overclaims in all the areas that ad technology claims to help solve, from the numbers of people they reach, and the management of frequency of exposure, through to targeting accuracies, and the attribution of effectiveness.

Knowing the current limits

It is vital for marketers to know that the communications planning mantra of "right time, right place, right person" still remains aspirational, and not yet a present technical reality, regardless of what vendors say. Let's look at a few examples:

- Ad exposure measurement
  The moveable feast that is an "ad impression" and how that depends on the point at which measurement happens in the traffic supply chain.

- Audience verification
  Over 50 percent of the internet is made up of non-human traffic (Imperva, 2022) which makes verification of ad traffic the necessity that it is. Often less spoken about are the natural limits of the measurement methods involved. JavaScript-based techniques, which yield the greatest amount of insight, are only feasible in certain environments. Image pixel-based techniques are a viable alternative but yield limited insights. IP and other list-based approaches are extremely limited and easily spoof-able.

- Reach and uniqueness
  Combined reach: to quote Marc Pritchard at the largest advertiser in the world, P&G (Procter & Gamble), "We have been talking about cross-platform media measurement for far too long" (WFA, 2019). Put simply, the industry does not yet have a solution for this, although there are ongoing trials and pilot programs being run in the US and the UK following a WFA-agreed framework (WFA, 2020). *Unique identifiers*: there are multiple ongoing industry initiatives to try and solve for identifying user identities in the age of privacy mandates and uniqueness of reach.

- Data and privacy management
  There is a plethora of media-owner-controlled "clean rooms" to house data, conduct analytics, and report on measurement. Having to work

across multiple media-owner solutions makes it harder to develop integrated measurement, manage frequency, and evaluate performance.

- **Frequency management**
  The promised management of frequency of exposure in digital campaigning currently verges on the mythical. Putting a limit on the number of impressions per user in a given period is 100 percent dependent on user identification and an assumed effective frequency requirement, both of which are dependent on a valid user ID mechanic, and a cross-media combined reach measure to facilitate any effective frequency modeling.

- **Targeting efficacies**
  Targeting is maybe the one fundamental area where programmatic overpromises and underdelivers. Contextual targeting, and brand safety and suitability measurement, are always a hop, skip and a jump from a brand reputation disaster. The most prevalent technique used to try to ensure that brands do not appear in inappropriate contexts is via the enforcement of keyword and URL lists, and the continuous, usually monthly updating of "block" and "allow" lists. A technique that allows for scale but is limited in potency. Other techniques that are based on semantic analysis of page content and using advanced language analysis are better, but far from scalable, plus they may be soon deemed illegal, as we will outline in a later chapter. Retargeting of users will also become illegal with the demise of cookies, whilst the use of contextual segments is making a return as a result (but the quality of them must be tested).

Partners and policies

The ability to understand what is described in the preceding pages is pivotal to good digital ad management, along with assessing your partner technologies in terms of what they can or cannot do in these terms, and being fully conscious of current industry-wide limitations.

Further, it is critical to develop a sense of whether those limitations are purely tech-driven or whether they come about because of ongoing policies of the technology partner in question.

The main type of artificially imposed limitation is currently policies surrounding data sharing. Some tech partners are more equal than others when it comes to their propensities to share datasets.

If data is the new fuel in the information age, we have had our own fair share of oil spills. Never has data been more important, and equally as potentially toxic.

The barriers to full and unfettered data sharing between technology partners, agencies, and brands, and between technology partners themselves, are usually an army of legal counsels on all sides. Everyone, on all sides, since GDPR and CCPA in 2018 and beyond, has gone through a legal arms race. The number of lawyers employed in AdTech has increased five-fold in the last three years alone, as has their understanding of the industry. Many of them have gone through a comparable form of accelerated learning vis à vis the mechanics of digital advertising. Large technology platforms have been successful in defending many of their transparency-restrictive policies towards advertisers by invoking user privacy as a roadblock, all the while generating significant revenue streams from the selling of user data to partner technology companies in the market.

It is important to develop an understanding of what any technology can give, beyond the hype of their B2B marketing efforts, as well as what technology partners are willing to offer from a policy as well as a tech perspective. This of course involves a bit of a process of continual education—an education that can be facilitated by truly independent advice, if and where necessary. And as outlined previously, the role of an agency partner in this specific context (one of independent technology advisor) is limited and cannot and should not be conflated with any other role they fulfill. Communications planning and media buying and independent technology advice are not mutually inclusive.

Software technologies are often centered around the automation of tasks, not the making of decisions. In a digital/intangible world it is more important than in the analog/physical world that humans comprise the majority of decision-making processes because the internet has far too much non-human input to be left without consistent and diligent human oversight.

Even the most efficient and sound technologies are only impactful when given the right task. It is easy to forget this in the intangible context of the internet because any malfunctions are equally intangible and invisible. For example, ad fraud is not a cybersecurity or bot detection problem, it is a counterfeit problem. This problem needs anti-counterfeit solutions and an anti-counterfeit mindset, not cybersecurity tools alone.

Most marketers, educated in the curriculums of communications, consumer behavior, microeconomics, macroeconomics, and sometimes specifically marketing, are not typically provided with the tools and information on how to navigate the impact of computer systems, internet servers, telecommunications, and broadband connections. That background should be a given before any ongoing assessment of partner value can be undertaken.

During a gold rush, sell shovels

The easy part of the value equation that most can grasp is cost, and the relative cost of doing business with AdTech suppliers is a perennial issue. What is not in question is that, for many suppliers, business growth since the advent of digital advertising has been nothing short of phenomenal. Like many a gold rush, fortunes have not necessarily been made in finding gold itself, but in the provision of necessary supplies to gold prospectors.

AdTech suppliers have grown in number like the shops, saloons, and brothels of countless mining towns of California in 1849, when real fortunes were made in supply-side businesses, as well as a good dose of chaos, disorder, and fraud. In a similar manner, the people who are really making money in modern marketing are the merchants of the goods and services required by prospectors.

Sam Brannan was one such merchant. At one time he owned the only store between San Francisco and the gold fields. He became rich not from gold prospecting, but from selling the goods required to prospect. At one point he capitalized by buying up all the shovels and pans he could for 20 cents each, and selling them for $15. He became the state's first bona fide millionaire. He was the Google of his day, not in the sense that Google is necessarily responsible for such a mark-up, but in the sense that, for many, Google is the only shop in town.

Which begs the question, how much money is being made, and what portion of advertising budgets is going to the modern-day equivalent of shovel salespeople?

Close to 85 percent of global digital advertising is now bought programmatically (Statista, 2022b). That means that only a small minority of digital ads are now bought directly without the aid of any third-party technology. This has been justified on the grounds of efficiency gains in targeting, relevance, and campaign controls.

In Chapter 2 we touched upon how much money makes it from advertiser to digital media owner. For every dollar spent on digital, at least 40 percent of your budget goes to technology partners and agency partners. Another 15 percent on top evaporates. Quite a "tech tax." There are very few industries on the planet that would accept a 50 percent-plus distributional fee, certainly not the adland clients of the past who were used to 15 percent commissions plus production fees only.

This of course is not counting for general wastage and fraud, and if we factor in quality metrics like the degree of viewability of the final ad, something close to 3–5 cents of your dollar might go to paying for real human eyeballs on your campaign, which is difficult to justify on the grounds of "efficiency gains." If you are the type of advertiser who wants uber efficiency as well as impact, sometimes these sums don't add up. Many tech companies that inhabit this space operate with very healthy margins. Google itself works on an operating margin of around 30 percent and revenues with continuous double-digit growth. Some of those margins have become challenged as they themselves face potential limits in the form of legislation and numerous monopolistic practice investigations.

Putting in place some guardrails

"Big Tech" in adland has so far successfully ensured that the industry, as well as national governments, does not impose guardrails on their own growth potential.

There are two types of challenges that they currently face:

1 Reviews from ad industry trade bodies: these include past and ongoing investigations into programmatic transparency from national ad associations like the US ANA (Association of National Advertisers) and their equivalents in the UK (ISBA) and Australia (AANA)

2 Investigations from national governments: these include ongoing investigations into potentially monopolistic practices amongst tech suppliers, by national governments across the globe.

These investigations face limitations of their own—both in terms of the digital literacies and skillsets of those involved, as well as limits to the technology being deployed to assist them. Both of which lead to taking time and effort, and the resultant two to three years to complete these studies is not surprising.

A moderate understanding of these technologies is becoming a prerequisite for intelligent deployment of advertising spend, and just as importantly, a necessary part of the armory of a modern marketeer as they face an onslaught of tech-savvy salespeople. Otherwise, there will be people queuing up to cash in on your ignorance.

If software engineers are the plumbers of the millennium, then data scientists will be the architects and building planners with purpose. And any ad professional who is skilled in the fundamentals of web technology and data management will be well placed to deal with any industry charlatans.

Marketers should be looked upon, and should look on themselves, as professional homeowners or building managers. Understanding how the infrastructure of their own operation is set up grants marketers the capability and confidence to tackle and conquer 90 percent of hurdles that have historically been outsourced to agents, consultants, and trade organizations.

Relying on an advertiser trade organization to provide guidance on how to procure the right ad technology, solve quality issues, and even optimize digital advertising campaigns, is like crowdsourcing plumbing solutions from your homeowners' association. Everyone's problems are different because everyone's habits, tolerance, and expected output are varied. With a wide-ranging spectrum of potential problems, relying on a centralized source for solutions is not an effective practice in the medium or long term. Problems and their consequent solutions do not exist on a linear plane. As the degree of complexity of the infrastructure rises, the subjectivity and malleability of solutions rises also. All marketers should look at their technology tools, platform licenses, and reporting interfaces as system components of the larger system of which they are custodians.

If all tasks and objectives are approached on a singular case-by-case basis, there will inevitably be friction between components of this system over time. The resulting positive and negative feedback loops between components must align in the intent of the marketer as well as the output of the system.

As we will touch upon later, it is often when existing or historical toolsets are very apparently not solving a new problem, that we look for shiny new objects in the market to fulfill those needs and aspirations. Better targeting, better conversion, increased ROI, increased ROAS (return on ad spend), increased tangible business outcomes, etc. are vague and lofty goals of marketing professionals that require the embracing of the mechanics of the system diagrams outlined earlier in this chapter.

The important thing to always keep front and center when trying to solve for improvement in metrics like frequency, cost, or quality, is that each of those comes with 8–10 contributing factors that must also be measured, analyzed, and worked on.

The internet is a dirty, messy place and we can often forget that as practitioners because of the intangible nature of successes and failures. We never actually see the mud under our metaphorical fingernails. The waste from a careless advertising operation with little oversight does not pile up like a landfill does. Intangible waste is ephemeral to the hundreds of data centers around the world, but the tangible monies in the accounts of the parties that facilitated it are very real.

Brand safety and suitability measurement in the digital ad world is a key example of where the limits of technology collide with the unrealistic expectations of public policy, moral virtue, and political activists. Anyone understanding the scale of content on the web, and the relative lack of control over where ads will eventually run, will understand how difficult it is to monitor the web page content of every possible context. For example, scraping words and images from pages and analyzing them at scale, with advanced semantic analysis over dozens of languages, is not only costly but, frankly, a myth. That is why all of the non-sample-based measurement of ad context is currently limited to URL string and keyword analysis and not the page itself.

Fraud detection is another one to get right up front and understand its limits. For any organization looking to address fraud exposure, whether that is advertisers, agencies or adtech trying to solve ad fraud, or banks, credit providers and insurance companies trying to solve financial fraud, it is important to take the following factors into consideration when devising a strategy to reduce exposure:

- What is the estimated volume of fraud occurrences across the board?
- What is the required coverage rate?
- What is the speed needed to get that coverage?
- False positive tolerance: What is the cost and impact of a mistaken fraud flag?
- False negative tolerance: What is the cost and impact of a missed fraud flag?

These factors will determine whether it is an exoneration-based or incrimination-based approach

When it comes to ad fraud detection, it's best to use an "exoneration" method; a source of traffic is "a bot until proven not."

Almost all verification companies in AdTech, though, tend to use an "incrimination" philosophy, which means they assume everything is "human until proven not." This can take a bit of time. Determining whether there are signs of robot activity spoofing human "mouse movements," for example, can take more than a few hundred milliseconds. And given that a digital trade (from automated bidding to the serving of an ad) can take no more than 100 milliseconds, some fraud detection happens far too late.

It's best to focus on checks that take a few milliseconds—and there are quick "exoneration" techniques in the market that can be deployed at scale.

The biggest misunderstanding that is perpetuated by most verification companies as well as the trade press in the marketing and advertising space is that "fraud follows the money." That could not be farther from the truth. While it is true that the most sophisticated perpetrators of ad fraud will always be experimenting with injecting counterfeit ad transactions from new or emerging media environments, like connected TV and gaming have seen since 2019, the majority of fraud does not.

Fraud does not follow the money; it rests on the path of least resistance, similar to how internet and telephone scams target the elderly and vulnerable rather than finance professionals or lawyers.

In the realm of ad fraud, it is the environments with the least technical resistance from fraud detection technologies combined with the environments and demand layers with the least diligence required to complete a transaction. In almost every business sector it is impossible to get fraud to zero, but the approach in effect should be a deterrent to those looking to make a few extra bucks as a side hustle, while also making the most sophisticated fraudster nervous about the consequences they could face.

Tech is only an enabler

Advertisers need technology to measure and verify digital ads because of the sheer scale, but a significant portion, fraud exposure, can be reduced not with technology, but with simple policy implementation and enforcement.

Requiring transactional transparency from sellers and brokers of media is the biggest piece of the digital advertising efficiency and effectiveness game. This means holding publishers, SSPs, and DSPs accountable for their data quality (completeness), transaction transparency, and commitment to providing value to their customers and vendors. If a marketer cannot rely on the sellers and brokers of the media they buy in to be honest, transparent, and diligent, then no degree of software, high-priced consultants, or technology procurement can improve that situation.

Without digital publisher transparency and diligence, there is no visibility into the quality of the traffic, media placement, or consumer attention that an advertiser is receiving from their investment. Measuring the results and outcomes of a marketing effort or ad campaign has a serious prerequisite, which is complete clarity and congruence in data expectations between the advertiser, the media owner, and the technologies those parties use. There is not a marketer in the world who is not compelled or required to measure, analyze, and report the ROI of media investment or advertising expenditure. The reason it is even referred to as an investment is because the rate of value return from the activity can be positive or negative, sort of like a gamble. The smart "investors" take systematic and methodical approaches to their media decisions.

Knowing the limits of software technology as a marketer is like knowing the laws of physics as an automobile engineer. Your task is to build the optimal engine and surrounding vehicle within the constraints of the system that it will operate in. For the auto engineer, that requires expertise in physics and familiarity with the driving experience; for the marketer, that requires expertise in internet protocols and a familiarity with ad platform features. No educator would ever recommend taking an exam without studying the underlying material or attending lectures. Similarly, no enterprise should force a marketer to take the exam of advertising in a live marketplace without being prepared on the underlying material. Mastering the foundational knowledge creates confidence in decision making and helps avoid mistakes from wasting time and effort on experimental technology that is not fit for purpose.

References

Imperva (2022) 2022 Imperva Bad Bot Report, https://www.imperva.com/resources/resource-library/reports/bad-bot-report/ (archived at https://perma.cc/HWW8-KQBB)

K2 (2016) Media Transparency: An independent study of transparency in the US advertising industry, https://www.ana.net/content/show/id/industry-initiative-recommendations-k2 (archived at https://perma.cc/36Z5-J36W)

Siteefy (2022) How many websites are there in the world? https://siteefy.com/how-many-websites-are-there/ (archived at https://perma.cc/8U52-JL35)

Statista (2022a) IOT (Internet of Things) connected devices worldwide from 2019 to 2021, with forecasts from 2022 to 2030, https://www.statista.com/statistics/1183457/iot-connected-devices-worldwide/ (archived at https://perma.cc/82AF-GVUV)

Statista (2022b) Distribution of digital advertising spend worldwide from 2017 to 2026, by purchase method, https://www.statista.com/forecasts/1316147/programmatic-share-digital-ad-spend-worldwide (archived at https://perma.cc/MCA9-CWUU)

WFA (2019) Global advertisers launch drive to establish cross-media measurement principles, https://wfanet.org/knowledge/item/2019/10/04/Global-advertisers-launch-drive-to-establish-cross-media-measurement-principles (archived at https://perma.cc/BXF7-2UC2)

WFA (2020) Establishing principles for a new approach to cross-media measurement: An industry framework, https://acaweb.ca/en/resource/establishing-principles-for-a-new-approach-to-cross-media-measurement/ (archived at https://perma.cc/YHG3-6QGZ)

Shiny new digital objects

06

Most marketers are drawn to new things. They enjoy finding new ways to engage with audiences or leveraging new pieces of technology.

There is also a natural tendency toward creativity in the industry. Even a CMO with a skew toward the analytical can have a secret and well-developed sense of creative innovation, all of which leads to a natural churn of ideas, continuous reassessment of assumptions and approaches toward going to market, with their doors naturally ajar to any technologist with a new platform to foster those new approaches. Most marketers are also just human. They crave known outcomes and comfort zones but sometimes fundamentally enjoy trying new things; it invigorates annual planning and stops everyone from getting bored.

Shock of the new

New tools, datasets, approaches, media platforms and publishers are constantly on offer. The digital advertising marketplace is naturally conflicted between using legacy tools for continuity and standardization, and new market entrants that have innovated beyond previous standards. There is a pattern to the resultant adoption of approaches and techniques, a cycle of sorts.

Gartner Research refers to it as a "hype cycle." A graphical representation of how any new things gain traction, spread, reach a "peak of inflated expectations," a "trough of disillusionment," and then basically find their balanced, productive place in our lives (Gartner Inc, 1995)

The current wave includes things like the metaverse, IOT, the accelerated adoption of AI (artificial intelligence) and ML (machine learning), with CTV (Connected TV) and NFTs (non-fungible tokens) approaching peak hype.

All of which may have a foundational role to play in all of our wider lifetimes, and/or little role to play in the world of advertising in the short term. Whilst AI-infused healthcare services may one day save millions of lives, a digital advertising example could be nothing more revolutionary than predicting what price to bid for ad space on xyz.com based on what the cost-per-click was a month before.

This hasn't stopped the digital ad industry from behaving like these technologies will revolutionize the industry, or advertisers from succumbing to SNOS, or "Shiny New Object Syndrome."

It's not a surprise that almost every enterprise AdTech software company currently touts an offering that includes, or is entirely based on, machine learning and/or artificial intelligence (ML/AI). The use of these terms, even to refer to regularly updated predictive modeling calculators, is helpful in fundraising for new technology upstarts, as well as in signing on new customers who have been tasked with incorporating ML/AI into their workstreams, which helps *their* managers check the boxes for their higher-ups.

It can also get addictive, and counterproductive. A perpetual cycle of adopting one new offering after the next without diligently finishing and assessing the first, and then quickly moving on again to the next shiny new thing. With advertising and media agencies happy to position themselves as visionaries and curators of newness to pander to such demands, there is a quarterly cycle of never-before-seen technologies made available for marketers to add to their toolkits. Especially given that they tend now to be in perpetual pitch mode, with the scale and velocity of pitch activity having increased two-fold in the past three years alone (Comvergence, 2020). In one year alone, advertisers concluded media reviews covering close to $30 billion in advertising spend.

Client relationships for agencies are less stable and long term. The industry increasingly incentivizes agencies strategically to offer new approaches that may or may not have been fully tested. Nor, as outlined in the previous chapter, are they fully owned by said agencies. VC-backed start-ups are touting AI-driven solutions, with agencies more than keen to adopt and present new offerings for overly keen clients; all of which is a recipe for a dysfunctional and partially sociopathic industry that adopts new phrases and technology as social currency with or without full comprehension.

Far too often, the folks who are selling these new tools are the least equipped to truly speak to the fundamentals of how the engine is built or how to maintain it. The market has accepted a category of service businesses to help customers use the already purchased software properly for their purposes. Sometimes these are third parties, but increasingly the service is offered by the company building the software itself. Both options come with pros and cons of their own, but all offer the promise of an innovative new way to connect with consumers and the digital marketplace.

The rise of the machines

But what if that digital market is increasingly non-human in its very nature? There are two fundamental understandings that all digital advertising practitioners need to have, in order to make informed decisions at every level:

1 50 percent of internet events (page loads, page views, clicks, form submissions, etc.) are now generated by non-human programs that operate on the web.

2 ~25 percent of new content on the internet in 2022 is created by non-human programs.

This means that 50 percent of events online are currently driven by bots, and 25 percent of content on the web is now written by bots. Things like jasper.ai, which "writes copy" for agencies, or the feature on Instagram/TikTok that has a computer-generated voice to narrate short clips where the human user has only entered text are recent examples. Understanding and embracing the prevalence of non-human presence in the internet experience will help avoid defaulting to advertising practices and processes that assume that humanity is behind 99 percent of creation and consumption online.

The impact of bots visiting pages or engaging with social media posts extends to the choices that actual humans make about what to read or watch.

The visit counter or curated list of trending content has a significant influence on what we decide to consume as a human collective. When reading and watching various things online, we spend 60 percent of the time scrolling a feed versus 40 percent on the expanded content itself. This data quantifies a social landscape where people can process current events from simply the text of the headlines themselves (HootSuite, 2022).

The industry is not shy in co-opting content creation innovations from elsewhere and pointing to their revolutionary potential for adland.

For example, "ChatGPT-3," the AI-driven conversational bot program that was launched in late 2022, is an example of something that has the clear potential to change fundamental parts of the advertising industry (and others). And Google themselves think of it as a potential game changer and a "code red" competitor for them (Grant and Metz, 2022). The capabilities that this open source tool is already demonstrating pose critical questions around just how much, for example, the search side of the online ad business could change if this tool itself is properly harnessed and monetized.

But therein sits the rub. Just how such an AI-driven chatbot can be leveraged by advertisers is a question that has yet to be fully addressed. There are clear implications for how such AI-driven tools could revolutionize copywriting and the creative industries, for example, but a viable path to sponsored bot-driven content is as yet unclear.

The wider concern is how these GPT (generative pre-training) models will be affected over time when fed non-human-generated data. The things that AI and big data software models are currently providing are often based on data that represents a lot of human activity. But with an increasing amount of text and posted activity on the web being generated by non-human programs, and not humans, the inputs for these tools are questionable and the future murky. Teams within OpenAI, the non-profit parent organization that operates the research for ChatGPT, are already discussing how to inform these generative models, and whether the source data they collect or analyze can contain "watermarks" that help determine whether it is bot- or human-created.

All marketers, media buyers, copywriters, and their colleagues should keep an eye on these types of software as their proliferation is inevitable, and their full impact unknown.

In many ways the growth of automated curation and distribution of certain types of content, and the willingness of both publishers and users to accept them, is leading to a clickbait content culture.

We often present it at conferences and client seminars as a mutually dependent ecosystem of the sea (social and content platforms), sport fishers (publishers), clickbait (headlines and thumbnails), chumbuckets (scrolling feeds), and eagerly biting fish (human attention).

The reason for using sport fishers in the analogy is that the fish are always thrown back into the sea after the bait is taken and the fish have been photographed, similar to being back in a scrolling feed after exiting the linked content. Over a long enough period of time, the bites become more valuable to the fisherman (publishers) than the fish (human attention) itself, in the same way that in a given food chain, the food that the prey eats will have an impact on the predator. Content, and therefore information, consumption has a similar chain of impact that can become toxic for all involved.

There have been numerous studies conducted by psychologists and government health departments on the significant impacts of embellished social media content on teenage mental health. The potential impact of misrepresentations or falsehoods (fake news) on adults is nothing short of that, often amplified by bot traffic pushing those pages into users' scrolling feeds or trending lists.

Having analyzed the real-world impact of this, the Center for Information Technology and Society (CITS) at UC Santa Barbara released and continues to update a diligently researched and thoughtful paper called "A Citizen's Guide to Fake News."

And having been called to task by activists and watchdogs on social media for helping monetize these inflammatory fake news sites, advertisers have relied on brand safety and content analysis technologies to help them avoid advertising on content determined to be unsuitable by a morality hive-mind. You can think of brand safety technology like a fact-checker program for full bodies of text, that needs to operate with 99.99 percent accuracy at a speed of over 100,000 decisions per second, based only on letters in the URL of the page in question.

As an industry, we have seen many erroneous assumptions around how, for example, content can or cannot be moderated for safe human consumption.

Similar to voices in the news around social or economic issues, it is often the extremes at the ends of the spectrum that find themselves amplified. Rational skeptics don't typically yearn for the spotlight.

Advocates of the monitoring technologies involved say they are sufficient, but most critics want them to do more, rather than less. If we consider again Tumblr's adult content ban in 2018, mentioned in the previous chapter, we can see how unrealistic aspirations of solving massive systems problems with shiny new tools can go wrong. The Electronic Frontier Foundation (EFF) made the following opening statement in their stance on the platform's policy:

> Tumblr's ban on "adult content" is a treasure trove of problems: filtering technology that doesn't work, a law that forces companies to make decisions that make others unsafe, and the problems that arise when one company has outsized influence on speech. It's also the story of how people at the margins find themselves pushed out of the places where they had built communities. And so, Tumblr is also a perfect microcosm of the problems plaguing people on every platform. (EFF, 2018)

Moderating content, and indirectly moderating or censoring speech, is a messy job that has been debated in the public forum since at least 2015. The work that the Brand Safety Institute, Sleeping Giants, and Check My Ads have done is testament to both the scale and durability of the problems that persist.

These debates centered around depicting social platforms like Facebook and Twitter as the modern town square that should or should not be limiting what someone can say, when, and to whom. The key difference is that the old town squares did not take every utterance from each citizen and carve it into stone for any and all to see for eternity.

Even newspapers were temporary and ephemeral in nature, given that there would be a new edition with new stories or updates to previous ones, on a daily, sometimes weekly basis. Nobody, except some of our grandparents and the subjects of hoarder reality shows, actually held onto newspapers and referred back to them at later dates. The impermanence of speech or content, and the fleeting nature of peoples' reactions, were critical to a collective detachment from any particular statement.

In our modern world, old statements in old contexts can be essentially teleported into a contemporary environment for judgment. Society is struggling with this dynamic and the solution is not in sight; our degree of willingness to raise pitchforks is directly correlated to what we currently collectively consider as monstrous today.

Brands will not be immune to this, so check your old tweets.

Blockchain: engineering vs. enthusiasm

There is a stark divide between those who have experience managing and constructing blockchain-based transaction ledgers, and those who have strongly advocated for it to be a panacea for the transparency woes of digital advertising.

Far too often from 2016–2021, distributed ledger technology (DLT) was dressed up or outright falsely labeled as blockchain. Distributed ledgers already exist across the systems of AdTech and are a primary cause of the confusion faced by many teams tasked with reconciling ad delivery on a monthly or quarterly basis.

Discrepancies in basic metrics like impression counts and unique user reach become a poisoned well for all subsequent analyses done across an organization; this is a bean counter's worst nightmare. If these peer systems across a supply chain cannot reliably count the same number of beans within 10 percent of each other, the expectation that they converge in agreement on the quality and details of those beans is merely wishful thinking.

Blockchain as a concept arose out of the distributed but immutable ledger technology created for bitcoin and other cryptocurrencies. Given the finite and invariable nature of total currency units across a system, this was critical to any further developments that proponents sought to build:

- a blockchain is tamper-proof, while distributed data can change;
- a blockchain is consistent, while distributed data is variable;
- a blockchain is accessible, while distributed data needs to be requested.

Let's try to agree that blockchain in its current state cannot be applied to digital advertising in its current state. The best that can be done is DLT intended for convergence: distributed ledgers of ad transactions across a publisher ad server, an SSP, a DSP, marketer ad server, third-party measurement, and third-party data provider, in respective declining counts by nature of the system.

The theory proposed by advocates of an AdTech blockchain purports that the aforementioned parties will collaboratively work towards contributing to a future common ledger that will be throned as a source of truth for the marketer. In practice, this means they will sacrifice their internal taxonomy for a common language and rebuild any and all processing pipelines accordingly. This is no small feat and will require a significant investment of time, effort, and something worth more than money: focused data engineering resources. Are marketers willing to foot the bill for that? Is the current state of affairs dire enough to warrant the investment? With all this disparate data, how can we establish the threshold of what can be considered "dire"?

Without a common taxonomy that provides clarity to all parties as a baseline, it is no surprise that not a single organization has embarked on a serious journey to re-engineer their data pipelines in this pursuit.

Blockchain technology and blockchain-inspired concepts can best be thought of as a shared accounting methodology. Right now, in digital advertising, everyone records their own numbers and then compares them when it comes time to bill. Distributed and corroborated ledgers will require that the parties in the supply chain all agree on the data before it is recorded to the ledger, so that when it comes time to do billing, there is no dispute over things like impression discrepancy.

Creating a mutually agreed-upon source of truth for where money was spent, and who took what, gives this concept amazing potential to have a positive impact on the media supply chain. What we see missing right now is the understanding that one party by themselves cannot implement blockchain technology on their media buying; it requires participation and cooperation from everyone in their supply chain. We've studied many blockchain-based companies, and almost all of the companies that are doing blockchain-related projects for advertising.

The most common factor that causes concern is that the companies don't always know who their ideal customers are, and the potential customers don't always know how using blockchain or distributed ledgers will actually help them. Going back to basics is key, and marketers would benefit from creating education cycles in their organizations to make sure their teams have a sufficient understanding of what the word "blockchain" means to them in the environment in which they operate today, and any future environments explored.

Assessing new tech: learn to speak geek

Most new digital objects have been created by software engineers.

Developers and engineers are usually two degrees of separation from the individuals they are building solutions for. The usual suspect that is translating back and forth is a salesperson or account manager.

It's important for the professional marketer to understand that the information they receive is rarely a first-hand account of the solutions being built. When we ourselves are working on how to equip marketers to be as successful in their roles as possible, we encourage them not to take a sales pitch as technical gospel.

Every ad professional should start by understanding the mechanics as well as the purpose of the piece of kit in question. If you're in charge of brand safety and suitability, or any related role, knowledge of a concept like the RTB (real-time bidding) protocol would seem essential to making informed decisions about things like vendor selection, coverage rate, and even cost of infrastructure. Similar to talking torque or horsepower (HP) with a car enthusiast, digital marketers should talk database speed or queries per second (QPS) with their technology suppliers. It is important, however, to treat technology suppliers like auto mechanics rather than fellow car enthusiasts because the supplier's goal is to sell you their car, not just share stories. In 2013, the National Bureau of Economic Research published a working paper called "Repairing the Damage: The effect of price knowledge and gender on auto-repair price quotes" which concluded that consumers can directly avoid price gouging and being taken advantage of by simply appearing well informed. Go figure!

Understanding the RTB protocol is like learning the rules of a multi-player board game. The better you know the rules, the less your success depends on strategically observing the subjective nature of how your opponents will act. This knowledge is unfortunately not prevalent in realms outside of specific engineering and product teams; it is often siloed from the true decision makers of how a company will act and respond to brand safety incidents.

Not wanting to get "into the weeds" can be a serious limitation and going beyond a surface understanding of technology in this regard is beneficial when assessing the tools and technology your agency is selling you. Marketers that spend time understanding the detailed rules of the digital game upfront may then naturally have to exert less energy on strategic planning around executions that are proven impractical. No brand wants to unwittingly waste precious time and resources on campaigns that can't be made manifest, or plans that die in the weeds.

Assessing new metrics: the rise of "attention"

A "website load request" from a user's device or browser is often the modern gateway to human attention. The most basic digital building block on that road to fulfilling David Ogilvy's first commandment of advertising: to sell. Vying for not only your precious human attention, but a short- or long-term purchase response.

The "attention economy" itself is now a bit of an overused phrase in adland, but there is little doubt that, if you are a media or platform owner, the only thing that matters is gaining, and maintaining, share of consumers' "time spent" with your platform. Any regular user of TikTok, for example, will testify to how "sticky" the user experience is in terms of time flying past. Engaging and relevant content always wins the "time spent" battle. And it is no surprise that in terms of *ad revenue per user*, the likes of TikTok are doing very well (an estimated $5 per user versus Facebook's $30) (Ku, 2021).

In a media world like TikTok where everyone is a media producer, there is an unlimited supply of ephemeral content. But there are only 24 hours in a day, with only a few of those representing opportunities to see ads. And there are seemingly endless content options available to those advertisers for where to place their bets on where they can most likely "borrow" someone's attention.

In Chapter 5 we referenced the claimed number of ad opportunities the "average consumer" is exposed to. No, we are not exposed to thousands of ads on a daily basis, but yes, there are thousands of daily "opportunities to see" out there.

The fact that we don't see them all is largely a result of human attentive capacity. It is not an unlimited commodity and at any given time we can only be actively aware of two to four things (Cowan, 2010). So yes, we can multitask, but we also have to build mental models to get through our average day, and that includes actively managing what we wish to be aware of. If anything, attention is primarily an active pursuit.

Time is truly precious, and it is the one factor that inhibits unfettered consumption of ads. There is a limit to the number of things the digital ecosystem can attentively "carry," as Donella Meadows would say. That's because attention sought in this ecosystem is of the voluntary human variety: "The carrying capacity simply means the number of growing things that can be supported by the environment over the long term. That is the sustainable number" (Meadows, nd).

Which begs the question, what is a sustainable number of new digital channels? Is there a natural trajectory for any new media, and when has it jumped the shark? These are fundamental questions that any media agency worth its salt can formulate answers to. They will do their best to justify reach and relevance for your brand along with measures of marketplace adoption or the reach of anything new, and the rate at which it is building. For example, if assessing the relevancy of a social channel, there are five main data points that are important to start with that will help differentiate its dynamics from other platforms:

1 The number of Daily or Monthly Active Users (only compare DAU to DAU, and MAU to MAU).

2 The Time Spent by Users relative to the DAU or MAU numbers (daily time for DAU, monthly time for MAU).

3 The percentage of pages/accounts where [# of Followers] > [# Following]:
   – this is essentially a statistical definition of content creator to differentiate from consumers or normal "users."

4 Percentage of User Time Spent in "Feed" versus navigated exploring of the platform.

5 X% of New Content vs. Y% of Old Content in User Feed:

- – is a user typically seeing recent posts, or are there a significant number of older posts/clips that end up in a user's feed?

What doesn't help is if those numbers come only from the entity in question, and not from a verifiable third party. Unsustainable and overly invasive data practices of third parties in AdTech have largely served as a scapegoat for why user network-based platforms have been able to keep prying eyes outside the walls; whether there is a garden inside or a swamp is only known by a select few custodians tasked with keeping it clean.

Attention is clearly a finite commodity, and many believe that it should be the new yardstick for the industry, and, at a stretch, the basis of value assessments, even a trading currency itself. We agree with them. Although sometimes it's akin to saying that you believe in world peace. You know it's right, and the noblest of goals, but it might never be attained. The economics of advertising trading does not yet value attention. It only values the opportunity for attention.

Impressions are a crude, reach-related measure. It is totally correct that not all "impressions" nor subsequent calculations of attention are equal. Viewability metrics produced by verification companies do help counter this and filter out those impressions that are essentially "unviewable." But definitions of viewability itself are often crude and simple as a rule. According to the MRC (Media Ratings Council), which organizes audits and facilitates guidelines to accredit measurement companies in this space, a digital display ad, for example, is deemed viewable "if 50% of the ad creative is visible for at least one second in the viewable space of the browser (MRC, 2022). Seeing half a display ad for one second. Or to be more accurate, half of the display ad must be "in view" for at least one second. Which is a critical distinction. The former assumes human involvement, the latter doesn't need a human to be involved for it to be true.

And therein lies the nutty problem—attention measurement involves tracking human participation. And often things like eye-tracking experiments in research settings are not very scalable, and the industry can only apply those sampled learnings in an extrapolated way to wider digital datasets. And as soon as we go down the path of extrapolation or modeling, we lose the thing that keeps the industry involved, especially from a currency perspective—*deterministic measures.*

And that ignores some purists in the psychological community who will claim that attention is only partially related to what we *see*. It's a selective and active thing, influenced by more than just the eyes—we attend to and see what we seek, and our eyes often don't see what's in front of them (Simons, 1999).

Attention measurement research is a noble effort, and very useful for planning purposes, but there is some way to go before it can be called a buying currency. The range of nuances in each buyer's definition and desire for consumer attention is unbound. If a currency were to be adopted at any significant scale it would have to overcome the significant political hurdles of each fundamentally different estimate-of-value in existing legacy approaches. If a marketer is at all relatively new to an organization, it is not straightforward to have their peers simply reject years of ingrained practices. Effecting change requires not only collective efforts across an industry with proper supporting evidence but often even more effort within an organization itself.

The metrics we choose to collectively use lead to a given set of incentives. As industry commentator Faris Yakob noted, this leads to "marketplace distortions":

"... the cost of an impression almost certainly does not properly price the increasingly scarce resource of chunks of aggregated human attention in the marketplace" ...

By his calculations, whilst TV looks expensive in CPM terms, it would be the cheapest way of buying attention, whilst the opposite is true for online video ads (Yakob, 2021)

The measurement of attention is a remarkably interesting topic but not one that yet lends itself to a simple agreed currency that media owners, for example, will accept. There are multiple, oft-competing approaches to the measurement of it across different platforms. Which in and of itself is an issue, as the industry already struggles with multiple companies offering an array of approaches to quantify the same thing. Even the MRC definitions of viewability have an alternative in the marketplace (WPP's own approach with slightly different definitions of viewability).

In late 2022 Havas announced they were incorporating attention metrics into all their planning. And therein is the point. It's a planning metric at the moment and a potentially powerful one. Not a buying metric.

When assessing new types of measurement and data, it boils down to assessing them in the context of their specific purpose. A trading currency has a very specific purpose and is often simply a convenient proxy for an agreed "truth." It doesn't always help if there is more than one.

The first rule of media research is always to be able to parse what is a currency, with a tenuous grasp on truth, and what is proper research. Plus, consume only the data you need, not everything that is out there.

Assessing new datasets: going on a data diet

New types of measurement, and new datasets, are persistently the shiniest of new shiny objects in advertising. The number of tech providers and agencies that promote their data-driven chops is countless.

We have all heard about how many terabytes and petabytes of data there are out there, and with things like the reduction in server costs, it means that in data terms, brands are currently living in an era of "all you can eat." We can all agree that data is big, and it's getting bigger, but making sense of data utility is not easy or consistent over time.

We need a healthy balance between data that is organic unstructured data, locally sourced goodness, and even some of the wild, free-range kind. That diet doesn't have to include the nasty, manufactured "aggregated" stuff. Nor the toxic illegal kind that can put brands in breach of privacy laws.

Where possible, data that is granular, privacy-safe, and broad in coverage is to be sought after. It has to be (1) smart (2) clean and (3) purposeful:

- **Smart data.** The data has to have context. It has to have labels that help give it sense. "Naked numbers" are pieces of data that have no context or sense. It's the very thing that led to the Mars Climate Orbiter disappearing into space (when there was a simple confusion in labeling between imperial and metric measures) (Dodd, 2020). Naked numbers are pervasive in digital advertising and pollute the ecosystem. Naming conventions and labeling systems are frankly all over the place. Brands and their agencies that do well operate strict naming conventions and encourage their tech partners to do the same.

- **Clean data.** Given that half of this ecosystem is driven by bots, there has to be a guarantee that the dataset you are optimizing against is completely free of signals based on bot activity. The current technologies that we have as an industry to help clean these datasets are what's known as "ad verification" vendors. As things stand, every vendor in the verification space uses different methodologies, different "training" datasets to come up with determinations of digital data stream quality—in terms of what is a bot, what is viewable, what is brand safe, etc. Some use samples, some don't and provide 100 percent coverage for a campaign. Given that verification costs come out of media budgets, they are not always deployed on all parts of a campaign. Some use probabilistic techniques and machine learning to augment their learning, some are totally deterministic. When different advertisers and their agencies use different verification vendors, different publishers, and different parts of the supply chain point to different sources of "truth," it can be a recipe for messiness. The digital ecosystem represents the largest and messiest dataset in history. Period.

- **Purposeful data.** Data needs to not only be accurate and complete, it also has to have purpose. It's important not only to be right, but also useful. At the most basic level, the purpose of a dataset is driven by who is paying for it, with data vendors supplying different sides of the supply chain. Each "sponsor" will often have very different motivations and objectives. The "buy side" in digital trading has different needs than the "sell side." Words like "optimization" are rife on both sides, and are overused in digital media. In essence, the central promise of optimization is one of taking a complete and clean dataset, deploying bespoke automated analytics, and making better decisions in line with given goals, at scale. Without clean data it doesn't work. Without full coverage it doesn't work.

As outlined in the earlier chapter on measurement, in some critical areas there is actually a data deficit. The data you need is not always available.

Different sectors will experience different propensities for data riches. Those in e-commerce, financial services and gaming, for example, are likely to have a rich trove of (consented) customer data. Compare this to the teams at brands whose customer contact is often through an intermediary such as a retailer, or automotive dealership, and the difference in the scale of the challenge facing such marketers becomes apparent.

There are also a lot of big CPG (consumer packaged goods) brands that have signed global contracts for DMPs and CDPs but they're starting to divest them because they're now reassessing their data strategies. They can't always just invent a new way of doing commerce, such as direct online sales, for the sake of fueling a database. On the other hand, many succeed at just that; for example, Adidas have created an incredibly robust owned and operated e-commerce strategy.

There are clearly new types of advertiser–retailer relationships emerging with the growth of retail media. There is always a need for bespoke additional data layers that fulfill transparency needs, and it is always better if it's an independent source.

A large part of assessing the viability of any new ad platform or publisher is therefore driven by ensuring that your preferred verification techniques and partners can be deployed. As we outlined earlier, there are limits to the capabilities of any technology, and that includes transaction verification techniques. What follows is an illustration of what types of media can and cannot be currently covered by these techniques:

- Open internet display
  Verification technology is able to track open-web display directly from an ad server. It provides advertisers with both a custom JavaScript tag and a custom image pixel to be implemented within the ad server across all relevant campaigns. Wherever it is possible for JavaScript to fire, the verification tag will fire and serve as the primary source of truth. In environments where JavaScript cannot fire, the image pixel will serve as a source of truth. The JavaScript tag collects significantly more data, but the image pixel is still able to perform rudimentary data collection. There are cookie-less solutions that are able to be deployed on all events that go through an ad server, and these will not have any adverse effects from the deprecation of cookies by Google/others.

- Open internet video
  Similar to display, verification technology measures video placements from within the ad server. The same image pixel and JavaScript tag implemented for display will also serve to track video. In environments where third-party JavaScript is permitted to fire (as in VPAID environments), the JavaScript tag will run and use the supplier's proprietary invalid traffic check to validate the impression. In implementations where third-party JavaScript is not permitted (as in most VAST environments), the image pixel will fire and instead of utilizing the standard invalid traffic check, suppliers often employ different methodologies to assess the device signature. The limitation of JavaScript to VPAID only is an industry limitation and not specific to any supplier.

- The Facebook internet, the Google internet
  All of the "major" social players (Twitter, Facebook, TikTok, YouTube, etc.) are considered walled gardens. As such they do not allow any third-party JavaScript to fire on their inventory. They may allow third-party

players to integrate into their code, but in that scenario the walled gardens maintain full control of what the third-party partners are able to see. At present there is no way for truly unbiased measurement within these walled gardens, but self-reported data feeds are available to all verification suppliers. For YouTube and other Google Internet placements, verification companies are able to utilize the image pixel in order to measure and verify impressions. All data is ingestible via YouTube's Ads Data Hub (which is now a prerequisite for any YouTube measurement). Facebook, Twitter and others do not allow for this, but landing page pixels can be implemented to monitor invalid click traffic (see below).

- **Connected devices**

  This fast-growing environment represents a challenge for measurement technologies. In order to prevent ad blocking, most OTT/CTV environments utilize server-side ad insertion (SSAI). By bundling up the content and the ads into one unit, SSAI creates a scenario in which users cannot block ads without also blocking the content. The consequence of this from a measurement perspective means that ad tags are not called in real time but collected at the start of a session and thus the measurable event is not actually occurring on a user's device. Most verification suppliers understand these limitations and for this format employ different methodologies to assess the device signature. Some also have developed unique approaches to measuring on CTV by curating a PMP which will only include transparent inventory that meets prefixed standards.

- **In-app**

  Similar to CTV, in-app is a rapidly growing and changing environment. For display most are able to perform full measurement due to the nature of how ads are served in-app. When an ad is served in WebView format, the measurement partner's browser technology-based checks are fully functional. To monitor valid app installations/opens, suppliers deploy JavaScript code within the app itself, which for example allows them to carry out a check of the capabilities of a user's device to ensure that the app is being downloaded/opened by a genuine user. In 2021, due to shifting privacy policies (i.e. the release of iOS 14), MMPs faced a significant degradation in their utility in identifying non-human traffic. The degree to which verification suppliers have been affected by this varies, with some being unaffected by this change in privacy and able to continue measurement of IVT in this space.

- Inbound traffic

  Outside of outbound campaigns, some verification partners are able to measure and verify the traffic of inbound campaigns by deploying JavaScript code directly onto a client's campaign landing pages. This implementation allows them to prevent waste inside retargeting campaigns, prevent pollution of analytics systems, and inform brands of non-human traffic within form submissions.

It is safe to assume that, for digital advertising, even the most diligent and precise operations have an exposure to low-quality or unwanted media of around 5 percent. Given the sheer scale of ad space enabled by an intangible and impermanent digital landscape, this can be assumed to grow proportionally with the budget of a particular advertiser.

Let's take a hypothetical CPG/FMCG brand, spending $1 billion annually on digital advertisements, and estimating an annual impression volume of 100 billion. With a conservative 5 percent error/fraud exposure we can estimate that $50 million of the spend is going to places outside of the marketer's intentions, but unintuitively more critical is the 5 billion ads that were placed and assumed to be viewed by people.

Those are 5 billion uncontrolled opportunities to create negative sentiment, consumer distaste, public backlash, or more sincerely, deliver financial benefit to parties monetizing material that is antithetical to the ethos of the marketer and their business. Depending on the brand, or the individual marketer, there will be either a moderate tolerance for those instances of misdirected ads, or a very low tolerance. Different brands have different expectations from their customers and the public at large.

If the only consequence is financial inefficiency, the job of the marketer is a bit lighter. If the tolerance is low, however, the marketer and their organization have perceived consequences beyond money, for ads going outside of the intended directions.

To truly have preventative measures in place as well as a crisis management plan requires complete transparency and first-hand access to the transaction data of the advertising that has been done. Most top 100 advertisers, by spend, do not have access to advertising data outside of the aggregate reporting made available by the platforms they use to buy it. This makes preventative measures possible only via the tools in the platform and makes crisis response a very uncertain exercise. The ideal state of a marketer should be to export smart data from the buying platforms being used and the clean data from their ad server on a monthly basis, normalize the exports, and combine that dataset into a repository of receipts with a common taxonomy. This dataset, even at the scale of 5 billion impressions per month, is not expensive to store nor is it overly difficult to query or utilize when the need arises. It is only when this clean data is collected and stored over time that it has the potential to be truly purposeful data to the brand, both for future media planning as well as crisis management.

It is not an easy task but responding to these incidents that arise on social platforms like Twitter, or even get written about in major press outlets, is only productive if you understand the technical reasons for how it could have been exposed. Apologizing for a mysterious occurrence and battling shame is a messy struggle and doesn't go well.

Measuring as much as possible is a good mantra and should be the aspiration of every serious marketer. But unfortunately it is not always the prerequisite to investment in new forms of media. If you are reading this book, chances are high that you are already a serious marketer or on your way to becoming one. A marketer that values diligence, transparency, and data-driven decisions will ensure that all investments in new media formats will keep the prerequisites of data hygiene and transparency top of mind even while simply experimenting with the new shiny object.

Assessing new media options: look before you leap

The rise of CTV (Connected TV) in the digital advertising sphere is proving to be a classic case of (i) the industry not learning from the mistakes of the past and (ii) measurement techniques not fully being in place before empires are built. Connected TVs are prime marketing real estate. The big screen captures the attention of viewers more effectively than a smartphone with a smaller screen. In addition, some ad spots have to be viewed before the show you want to watch appears, which almost guarantees your attention. The device and channel owners are generating growing amounts of data on viewing behavior, which leads to claims of "better ad targeting" with associated higher prices, but also fatter rewards for those who can cheat the system. CTV advertising is the fastest-growing channel in terms of YOY growth (Morgado, 2020), and it's also officially the epicenter of fraudulent activity.

Unfortunately, the business empires being built around CTV as a media format are not measurement friendly for third-party technologies. SSAI (server-side ad insertion) is a technique for delivering an ad that effectively

Figure 6.1   The trading and delivery systems when gamed

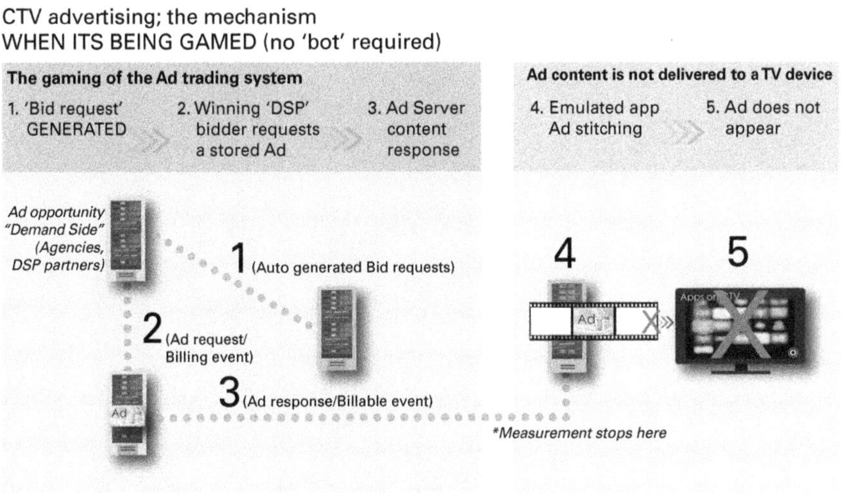

CTV advertising; the mechanism
WHEN ITS BEING GAMED (no 'bot' required)

stitches ad content in with the stream of the program in question. They are bundled and delivered together. Whilst this is great for the end-user experience, guaranteeing better overall streaming quality, it's not great for those in the ad industry who want to verify and measure the quality and veracity of claimed audiences. In many ways the industry is at the mercy of the channel owners and SSAI server gatekeepers, none of whom have a vested interest in demonstrably opening up to independent measurement.

It's also a system that can be easily "spoofed." This is where, for example, those claiming to have found great CTV audiences and charging CTV prices are actually just dressing up audiences from cheaper media. Getting the industry to think they are buying CTV audiences, when they might just be on a phone app, is not proving difficult for the spoofing community. The spoofing is akin to getting a pizza delivered to a posh neighborhood, but not necessarily directly to a valued customer's door. The supplier of that pizza can only track when a neighborhood guard got the pizza, not when the customer got it.

All advertisers using machines and algorithms to buy space on connected TVs are affected. From our own estimates, anywhere between 5 and 80 percent of programmatic TV inventory available in exchanges on a given day is fraudulent. The number of CTV fraud impressions detected more than tripled last year and is now in the hundreds of millions. A byzantine supply chain obscures the link between the ultimate buyer and seller, opening a window for fraudsters to game the system.

Figure 6.2   Spoofing the CTV system without any ad delivery.

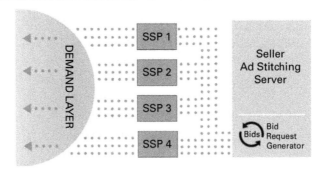

It's a problem that is far more complex than the waves of digital ad fraud that arose more than a decade ago, when fraudsters generated billions of false clicks on online ads. A fake click can be compared to a real one, but ad views are more ephemeral.

Our own research points to how easy it is to game this system, and in 2021 we published and released a research report called RapidFire in reference to the way that counterfeit CTV ad requests are blasted toward bidders like a rapid-firing projectile machine. We listed some key findings in the executive summary of the report:

- 50 percent (+-3%) of CTV traffic available (made available for auction) in exchanges is counterfeit.
- 80 percent of counterfeit CTV traffic sellers have four or more entry points into exchanges.
- 15 percent of counterfeit CTV traffic sellers have their own operational seller seats on exchanges.

The obvious question posed to us by journalists, trade association leaders, and clients alike, was why existing verification approaches are missing this. We answered this by pointing out that existing approaches are not factoring in the new intermediary in the process, which is like a holding area in a different location. Traditional ad-verification technology approaches have not been able to catch this because they rely on being able to flag invalid user agents and IP addresses via the bid stream. Since the growth of CTV is undeniable, it is vital for the industry to move away from using web-based checks that do not translate to the CTV SSAI environment. IP addresses in bid requests will be of the user, but the IP seen by the ad server will be of the

SSAI server. We must stop relying on IP addresses in order to ensure proper measurement in CTV.

The tools currently available to the advertiser to deal with this growing and difficult problem face some real challenges in releasing CTV-focused solutions without overcomplicating the ad operations workflows or compromising their core offerings for display and web video ads.

Assessing new tools: ones with purpose

There are always shiny new objects available on the market that are promoted as the silver bullets to age-old problems.

Think of infomercials from the 1990s and early 2000s. A cheap, simple solution to pet hair on the sofa, which means you don't need that weird sticky plastic cover anymore! A new, improved laundry detergent that fights stains 10 times stronger than whatever mediocre detergent you've been using till now! A suction cup with a handle that removes dents from your car or motorcycle, potentially saving tens of thousands in repair bills!

Shiny new objects are very rarely meant to address the cause of problems, only the symptoms. What can really make it easier to get pet hair off your sofa? Don't have a cloth sofa if you have pets that shed (obviously nobody would suggest replacing your existing furry family member for a hypoallergenic pet). What can really help prevent stains in your clothes? A diligent laundry regimen where the dirtiest clothes are addressed early to prevent stains from setting in. What can prevent a lifetime of repeated dents and associated costs with your vehicle? More careful driving or better insurance.

The issue with real systematic solutions to big problems is that they are hard to package in a neat box to sell uniform commodities to a large body of customers. This is usually where consultants come into the picture! Unfortunately, it is rare to find consultants or consultancies with objective takes on the technologies that their strategies are paired with. They are either restricted to making the most of existing procured technologies, limited to recommending the handful that they have direct experience with, or their organizations have preferred technology recommendations as part of a larger partnership or alliance. These combined factors make it complicated, messy, and frustrating to make confident, informed choices on what technology best *assists* an organization in tackling a problem.

Note we said *assists*, not solves. Technology can only do the specific task it is designed and deployed to do; a task that is just a part of a solution set. Having the "best" ad server in the market doesn't make it so that your advertising will be efficient. You need good publisher diligence and a well-monitored DSP to really ensure that, but having a solid, reliable ad server is a great thing!

When "one problem" seems to require multiple solutions, it is more likely than not that your problem is multifaceted and has a list of contributing factors. Dynamic creative optimization will not fix advertising efficiency if you have not already addressed industry-standard problems around transparency, quality, reporting, and billing.

Just as we all know of "industry-standard solutions," there are underlying "industry-standard problems" that inspired the rise of those companies and led to a market for investing in the proposed solution. With industry-standard problems there is an apathy that can develop over fatigue from the same press headlines, conference panels, and company lunch and learns. If it's happening to everyone, is it really "happening" to anyone?

We understand that just keeping the train moving can seem daunting and overwhelming on its own. As builders of a startup, we know that even teasing out conversations around efficiency can make people feel ill when day-to-day deliverables are not running as smoothly as desired. Welcome to corporate business life! Aren't you glad you got that degree, or two?

Tools should be assessed against specific purposes. The most effective way to approach a solution search is by mapping out all aspects of the problem being faced as a system with components. Think back to the limitations of technologies we covered in Chapter 5, and we'll revisit the frequency cap for this scenario.

The easiest, most painless path for a leader to solve frequency cap problems is to find a company that sells an attractively packaged box called "Best Frequency Cap Solution."

The more diligent leader, with an affinity for punishing themselves with boring bidder mechanics for two full days, would gather their team and assign each of them to address each of the components of the Advertisement Frequency Per User system:

- One person oversees identity data platforms, and the integrity of the data that is being ingested or utilized.

- One person would be a liaison to legal/compliance to have regular (likely quarterly) discussions on how liberal or conservative the company should be with its definition of uniqueness; the more conservative they choose to be, the more disclosures, disclaimers, and indemnifications are going to be required by the legal and compliance colleagues.

- Another person on the team would have to maintain subject matter expertise on the speed and cycles of DSPs and other ad technologies updating their records of ads served to a particular UUID (unique user identifier).

Now think back to the neat box with the ribbon and label: wouldn't that be easier? Would it work? How would you know if it isn't working once deployed? In the AdTech space, shiny new objects often lead to attempts to solve problems of opacity with more opacity in the form of paying for another party's view of the target information. These solutions don't often last very long and if there are not tangible results or efficiency gains from a procured technology, loss of faith from regime change can make it difficult to maintain customer retention or address new solution needs with existing budget limitations.

The thing about shiny new objects is that within a reasonably brief period of time, the shine and the newness fade and it becomes just another object. Procuring new technologies that fit your needs and purpose in the present as well as the future, is the only way to avoid buyer's remorse with software licenses. Marketing and advertising budgets being fixed for a fiscal year means that every penny spent on software means a penny less to spend on actual media and customer messaging. Over time, the successful marketer will have a fairly lean toolkit of core competence, with space for tools that are auditioned for specific purposes but not necessarily kept for the long term. Wise and conscious marketers will not shy away from new tools or shiny objects, but will know that not everything that glitters is gold. All new objects must be examined for purpose, diligently tested, and only kept if the vision of future utility is as strong or stronger than the present-day use case.

The costs of flying blind

The moment a user requests some content online, immediately there are hundreds, if not thousands of advertisers bidding for their attention. A supplementary and secondary "trading economy" in and of itself, an algorithmically driven, hidden economy, which is more akin to financial market trading than it is market-stall trading: opaque, complex, and often misunderstood.

The grand promise of programmatic trading is to utilize technology to manage this "trading economy" to solve the challenges of that "attention economy" for the benefit of brand owners—who, being only human, suffer from the same demands on attention that we all do. "I don't have to know how it works, just show me that it works," which is a somewhat Faustian bargain.

The Federal Trade Commission (FTC) in the United States, self-attested to be responsible for "Protecting America's Consumers," has been routinely vocal and thoughtful in its observations of the online advertising marketplace, with many previous initiatives becoming increasingly relevant over two decades.

In March 2000, former Commissioner of the FTC, Sheila Anthony, gave a speech at the American Bar Association titled "Advertising and Unfair Competition," where she outlined the FTC's national advertising program (FTC, 2000).

In the early portion of the speech, she described that:

> In any dynamic environment, some level of consumer confusion is inevitable. Confusion is increased by new market entrants who are uninformed about basic principles of advertising law. In addition, the unscrupulous marketers are clever and quick to exploit and mislead consumers.

When speaking about how the FTC will enforce solutions, the former Commissioner said that:

> Two areas that have received increased attention are liability and remedies. Advertisers are responsible for all claims, express and implied, that are reasonably conveyed by an ad. Advertising agencies can also be liable for deceptive advertisements if the agency was an active participant in the preparation of the ad, and if it knew or should have known that the advertisement was deceptive. In addition, it is well settled that retailers can also be liable for false and misleading claims, but we generally will not hold them liable if they reasonably rely on the manufacturers' substantiation. Companies can also be liable if they provide others with the "means and instrumentalities" for engaging in deceptive conduct.

Getting increasingly more poignant throughout her speech she starts her closing remarks with:

> Tough and vigorous law enforcement remains a top priority in our internet efforts. Since September 1994, the Commission has brought over 100 internet-related cases. Many of these involve traditional scams in a high-tech venue. For example, the internet has provided especially fertile ground for pyramid schemes and other get-rich-quick ventures. Increasingly, however, the technology is enabling the scam itself.

Commissioner Anthony also revealed that while consumer privacy was a leading concern of regulators, with 22 years of market history and technical development as hindsight, it is surprising to see how accurate some of the FTC's perspective turned out to be and how wrong other predictions were. Agents of advertisers can be held responsible for deceptive advertisements if involved with creating the ad and unfortunately for some agencies and their tech clients in the future, the reality that B2B advertising is also subject to these rules will come as a hard pill to swallow when negotiating their fines with regulators.

Flying blind and assuming that software products work exactly as advertised or pitched in a presentation can have severe consequences for the efficacy of an advertising campaign from a lack of oversight and regular monitoring. The diligent marketer will routinely find success by not only avoiding falling victim to false or exaggerated claims, but also by approaching every campaign launch prepared for snafus galore. Maya Angelou very wisely wrote, in her renowned autobiographical work *I Know Why the Caged Bird Sings*, "Hoping for the best, prepared for the worst, and unsurprised by anything in between."

The total cost to an organization from a failed marketing initiative is not only the money that went into funding the planning, media, and execution, but also includes the opportunity cost of the missed ROI of a squandered success.

In order to buy and sell access to human attention, a currency is needed. As we outlined earlier, the most basic currency is the impression, an inherently fluid beast and only a measure of an ad being served. There are, as yet, no attention-based metrics that have gained industry-wide traction, although some are trying (Amplified Intelligence, 2022)

The metrics we use to trade, our KPI's, naturally create incentives for the suppliers in the market. We mentioned that pre-bid viewability was one of our favorite examples because it also applies to the issue being described here. Measured viewability started as a buyer KPI that eventually became a seller incentive because the burden of viewability was outsourced to the brokers/agents that sat in the middle. The opacity of the programmatic media buying ecosystem makes the market ripe for, and rife with, fraud, creating marketplace distortions in asset valuations. Combined with trading opacities, a prime ingredient for a thing that one author (Hwang, 2020) has described as a looming "Subprime Attention Crisis." Bad asset valuations, trading opacities, perverse incentives, and minimal industry self-regulation. Boom and bust, market bubble cyclical mechanics writ large. No media planner would ever get fired for directing their budget toward Facebook or Google ads, the widely inefficient but safe path with reputational guardrails. This strategy of bowling down the lane with guardrails prevents outright failure, but does not guarantee any real success for an advertising strategy or specific campaign.

Why is this happening? For one, we have all bought into the myth of the potency of some digital ad targeting techniques, and their associated digital demons: cookies and behavioral profiles. There is solid evidence that ads targeted with cookies generate only slightly more revenue than ads targeted without cookies (Tkacik, 2019). Even non-cookie-based techniques have yet to fully prove their worth. The ICO (Information Commissioner) in the UK itself effectively couldn't find any evidence that the whole Cambridge Analytica psychographic targeting actually worked (ICO, 2020). On top of this, we have bought into the myth that more data makes ads more effective. The role of data in advertising in itself has gone through hype cycles within hype cycles, tech optimist and tech pessimist circles. Ad tech is not as good as the former think, and Mark Zuckerberg might not be as evil as the latter think. More data does not mean better advertising. If anything, it's about time that brands went on a "data diet," with some industry observers and policies even advocating an organized hunger strike against the data brokers. The consumer data marketplace and the behavioral data marketplace were mashed together in the name of consolidation and mergers, but are wildly different beasts in their nature and in their practice.

References

Amplified Intelligence (2022) Attention Research Findings 2017–2022 https://www.amplifiedintelligence.com.au/wp-content/uploads/2022/07/Amplified-Intelligence-Attention-Research-Findings-2017-to-2022.pdf (archived at https://perma.cc/RS9A-DTHT)

CITS (2022) A citizen's guide to fake news, https://www.cits.ucsb.edu/fake-news (archived at https://perma.cc/GU7T-TGSX)

Comvergence (2020) "It's more transformational": For the third time in five years advertisers will launch a mediapalooza of account reviews, https://comvergence.net/2020/09/for-the-third-time-in-5-years-advertisers-will-launch-a-mediapalooza/ (archived at https://perma.cc/3M34-RQD8)

Cowan, N (2010) The Magical Mystery Four: How is working memory capacity limited, and why? *Current Directions in Psychological Science*, **19** (1), pp 51–57, https://www.ncbi.nlm.nih.gov/pmc/articles/PMC2864034/ (archived at https://perma.cc/ND36-YH6P)

Dodd, T (2020) Metric vs imperial units: How NASA lost a 327 million dollar mission to Mars, *The Everyday Astronaut*, https://everydayastronaut.com/mars-climate-orbiter/ (archived at https://perma.cc/L6YW-3F4H)

EFF (2018) What Tumblr's ban on 'adult content' actually did, https://www.eff.org/tossedout/tumblr-ban-adult-content (archived at https://perma.cc/PT5P-4PZU)

FTC (2000) Advertising and Unfair Competition, https://www.ftc.gov/news-events/news/speeches/advertising-unfair-competition (archived at https://perma.cc/3FUB-W84Q)

Gartner Inc (1995) The hype cycle model explains a generally applicable path a technology takes in terms of expectations or visibility of the value of the technology (y-axis) and time (x-axis). See https://www.gartner.com/en/research/methodologies/gartner-hype-cycle (archived at https://perma.cc/DFP4-5RA9)

Grant, N and Metz, C (2022) A new chat bot is a 'code red' for Google's search business, *New York Times*, https://www.nytimes.com/2022/12/21/technology/ai-chatgpt-google-search.html (archived at https://perma.cc/J2HF-6CZA)

HootSuite (2022) Global State of Digital Report, https://www.hootsuite.com/resources/digital-trends (archived at https://perma.cc/D9MT-Z676)

Hwang, T (2020) *The Subprime Attention Crisis: Advertising and the time bomb at the heart of the internet*, FSG originals

ICO (2020) Letter to Julian Knight MP, Chair of the Digital Culture and Media and Sport Committee, chrome-extension://efaidnbmnnnibpcajpcglclefindmkaj/https://ico.org.uk/media/action-weve-taken/2618383/20201002_ico-o-ed-l-rtl-0181_to-julian-knight-mp.pdf (archived at https://perma.cc/A5HV-QMPV)

Ku, D (2021) Which social media platforms make the most revenue? *PostBeyond*, https://www.postbeyond.com/blog/revenue-per-social-media-user/ (archived at https://perma.cc/8MK5-TEH6)

Meadows, D (nd) The Donella Meadows Project: Academy for Systems Change. https://donellameadows.org/ (archived at https://perma.cc/ZNV3-7JEG)

Morgado, M (2022) Netflix – What can advertisers expect? *ebiquity*, https://www.ebiquity.com/news-insights/blog/netflix-what-can-advertisers-expect/ (archived at https://perma.cc/XEJ7-R4N9)

MRC (2022) Standards and Guidelines Summary, https://mediaratingcouncil.org/standards-and-guidelines (archived at https://perma.cc/XHN8-QAM2)

Simons, D J (1999) Gorillas in our midst: Sustained inattentional blindness for dynamic events, *Perception*, **28** (9), https://journals.sagepub.com/doi/10.1068/p281059 (archived at https://perma.cc/AF8H-NW65)

Tkacik, D (2019) Ads, cookies, and the European privacy regulation, Carnegie Mellon University, https://www.cylab.cmu.edu/news/2019/07/08-european-privacy-laws.html (archived at https://perma.cc/AES9-KJJS)

Yakob, F (2021) *Paid Attention*, Kogan Page

Understanding your leverage 07

As advertisers, just how much power do you currently have?

Traditionally, advertisers have gained leverage based on the sheer negotiating clout associated with their budgets. The size of a national ad budget went, and still does go, some way to getting the best terms from national media owners. Local agencies pool these monies with other brands, and even greater terms are gained. That has been the traditional modus operandi of buying leverage.

That, in many ways, has also led to the legacy structures that still exist in the industry today, with agency holding groups built on the immediate value of pooled leverage, and local pitches being won and lost based on what an agency "can versus could" do for a brand in that market.

The digital era has upended most of that. Digital advertising is now the largest single channel to invest media in, and the largest media owners are not national but international. Most agency pitches are rarely local affairs, and money doesn't always guarantee good terms.

The original promise of the internet advertising landscape offered an efficient and fair ecosystem regardless of the size of your budget. But then the big platforms arrived.

Elephants outside the boardroom

The digital advertising industry's biggest names are currently Alphabet (Google), Amazon, Apple, and Meta (Facebook), with others waiting in the wings to take advantage of dollars going into established and newer forms of digital spend. New entrants will include channel options from the likes of Netflix and Microsoft, as well as the rise of retail media off the back of an e-commerce explosion. All of which pose challenges for the buy side.

Google and Meta alone will strategically capture the rainfall of more than 50 percent of all ad monies this year (Zippia, 2022). Together with

Amazon, they collectively account for more than $7 in every $10 of global digital advertising spend (74 percent, up from 67 percent in two years, whilst the rest of the online ad market is growing at a combined growth rate of 3 percent year-on-year in comparison, which is slower than the rate of inflation) (eBiquity, 2022)

Things don't always stay the same, and markets change. In many ways, Google has an unhealthy dominance in the market as things stand. This is largely a result of their original search business, acquisitions like DoubleClick and YouTube, but it also comes significantly from the dominant market position they maintain in the "delivery piping" of internet advertising.

The original promise of software disrupting the ad trade in a utopian manner has simply led to the growth of exceptionally large, dominant intermediaries. They increasingly own the industry. They can exert power in the industry beyond the reach of any traditional media owner. And on the face of it, they offer the buy side of the industry little leverage.

So, what can an advertiser do when faced with such might? There are four things that we will touch upon here. Things that attempt to curtail platform power, some of which you can control and some you cannot:

- the leverage being exerted by statutory authorities;
- the platforms being at odds with each other;
- the inherent leverage of you and your partners;
- cross-industry self-regulation (trade groups).

Masters of their domains

No one has quite dominated the digital advertising scene like Google and Facebook.

From the moment Google first appeared in 1998, with an original way of ranking the relevance of search results, the ad industry changed. The rankings that it gave to websites, and the opaque algorithm that drove those rankings, became the foundation on which Google went on to dominate the gateway to internet usage—via the search box.

No one knows our secrets quite like the Google search box knows our secrets. It became the de facto dataset that reveals our intentions, both at an individual level and, arguably, at a societal one.

It could be gamed, of course, and a sub-industry of "search engine optimizers" evolved to try and ensure that a Google search would rank their clients' pages more highly. Not "advertising" in the classical sense, but certainly in the domain of media agencies

In the early days, Google almost positioned itself as a pure play independent arbiter, pointing to the "vested interest" of any advertiser-owned web properties. And transparency was the cornerstone on which this behemoth was founded: "We believe the issue of advertising causes enough mixed incentives that it is crucial to have a competitive search engine that is transparent and in the academic realm" (Brin and Page, 1998).

But once they were over this initial moral high ground, and as more people used it, the "database of intentions" they had effectively built was milked and monetized. And no one has quite monetized the way Google has monetized. It's a platform, and an associated SEO industry, that has sucked up traditional advertising and promotional budgets as a result.

It could be argued that it has peaked as a potent search tool—beyond the first few results of any search (the ones that are clearly overt ads), the rest are SEO results filled with affiliate links and hidden ads (Brereton, 2022). The results can be a bit bland and expected. A bit beige. Vanilla. And it's not always clear if that is a result of weakness of the Google algorithm, or just how good the SEO industry is at gaming the results.

And there is some evidence that the rise of retail media is beginning to impact this core foundation of the Google empire. Search, as a consumer behavior, is as strong as ever. However, it's where consumers conduct their searches that is driving change—many are just doing their searches in Amazon itself. That is where brands buy keywords or result placements.

But Google still dominates the search industry as much as Facebook has dominated social outreach. And both have seen off genuine alternatives and are continuously asked to. They have been a necessary tax for anyone contemplating search and social campaigning for years. Like tolls that run right along the highway of the media buying industry.

There is nothing wrong with having a strong market share within your vertical.

But in many ways, these tech giants can seem like the traditional industries of Japan. The original "keiretsu" and "zaibatsu" included Sumitomo, Mitsui, Mitsubishi, and Yasuda. They were all horizontally and vertically integrated—not only dominating their chosen businesses, but also controlling extensive supply chains and raw materials, with their industrial and financial sectors joined at the hip. They were, and their modern offspring are, economic groups that are influential across the board, and provide significant economic stability.

Countries like the United States have always accused keiretsu groups of unfair business practices aimed at shutting down foreign competition. Their monopolistic tendencies have at least been partially that—defensive mechanisms to avoid foreign takeovers.

So, too, in adland, we currently have a number of dominant, but defensively minded, behemoths. Whilst there may be nothing wrong with Japanese industry protecting itself from overseas takeovers, in digital adland with its global footprint, there is a lot wrong with being overly "horizontally and vertically" integrated. Especially if you want to avoid industry regulators.

Google, for example, doesn't just offer a search engine business. The extent of its influence across digital advertising is illustrated in Figure 7.1.

Given this type of dominance, Google's AdTech business has been accused of an array of abuses. Accusations have included things like making it impossible for rivals to partake in the siphoning of money from publishers—all of which have been of course contested.

Not up for debate though are the facts that (i) advertisers' hands have been somewhat tied for a generation, and (ii) there have been a growing number of calls from lawmakers to investigate the company.

Statutory authorities playing catch-up

This horizontally and vertically integrated dominant position is drawing the attention of regulators across the globe. Google is in a world of trouble with governments everywhere since countries in every continent have either filed lawsuits or have started probes.

Monopoly and antitrust inquiries include:

- US: marketplace lawsuits, alleged abuse of data access, accused collaboration with Facebook on data deals that maintain dual monopoly.

- UK: the Competition and Markets Authority opened an investigation into the practice in digital advertising known as "header bidding." It goes to the heart of how Google makes its money. Alphabet faces lawsuits over anti-competitive digital advertising practices and over-pricing app store purchases.

- European Union: officials are looking into whether Google's anti-competitive practices have harmed app developers. The company has been fined for stifling competition through the dominance of Android. The EU has already fined Google more than $8.2 billion in recent years over antitrust practices.

Figure 7.1 The Google tech stack for both buyers and sellers

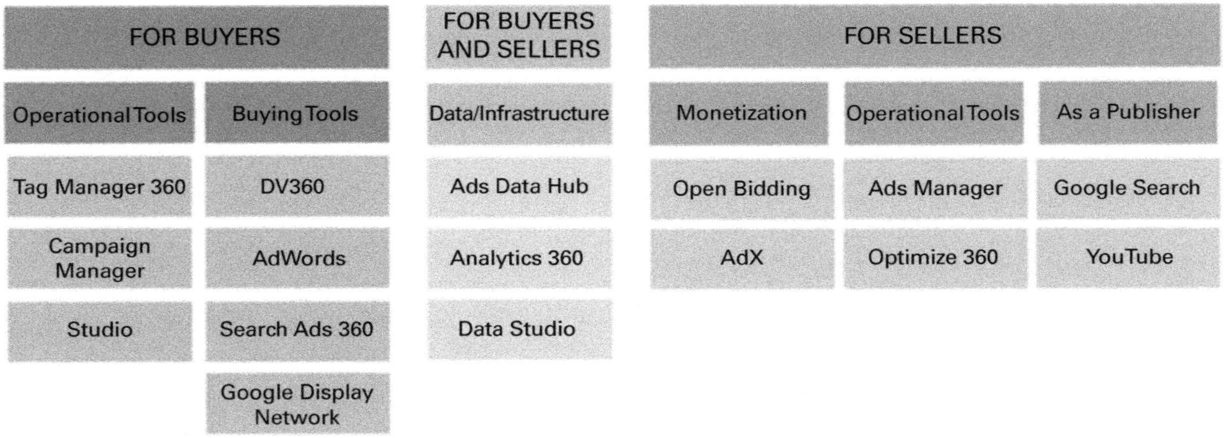

FOR BUYERS		FOR BUYERS AND SELLERS	FOR SELLERS		
Operational Tools	Buying Tools	Data/Infrastructure	Monetization	Operational Tools	As a Publisher
Tag Manager 360	DV360	Ads Data Hub	Open Bidding	Ads Manager	Google Search
Campaign Manager	AdWords	Analytics 360	AdX	Optimize 360	YouTube
Studio	Search Ads 360	Data Studio			
	Google Display Network				

- Australia: there is also an ongoing ACCC (Australian Competition and Consumer Commission) inquiry into digital marketplace practice.
- South Korea: Google is also being investigated for potentially violating South Korea's rules governing in-app payments.
- India: the Competition Commission of India has penalized Google for monopolizing its Play Store payment system, and for abusing its dominance in the Android ecosystem.
- Netherlands: apart from a lawsuit over its digital advertising practices, Google is also embroiled in a probe over its app Play Store payment rules, similar to the ongoing Indian case.
- Indonesia: an antitrust agency is probing Google for potential unfair business practices over its Play Store payment services.
- Japan: an ongoing investigation is determining whether Google has unfairly leveraged its dominance over the markets for phones, smartwatches, and other wearables.
- South Africa: a competition commission has made provisional recommendations for how Google should display search pages, to better distinguish between paid advertising and traditional organic search results.
- Canada: the Competition Bureau is seeking more information on whether Google behaved in anti-competitive ways in the online advertising industry.

Data privacy and policy issues:

- Australia: a court ordered Google to pay $43 million in penalties for misleading users on collection of their personal location data.
- South Korea: a privacy commission fined Google $50 million for violating privacy laws, using data from other websites as well as apps to generate customized advertisements.
- Italy: an antitrust inquiry is investigating whether Google has abused its dominant position by hindering data portability rights.

Copyright and content infringement issues:

- France: Google paid $528 million in fines to resolve a dispute related to news publishers displaying copyrighted content.
- Germany: the German government is examining Google's content licensing deals with news publishers and its data processing terms.

Being successful is a risky business. The large, dominant platforms have been associated with exponential revenue growth and increasingly some industry and legislative guardrails. But how effective are industry and governmental efforts at taming the beasts?

In late 2022, Google was fined almost $400 million in the US's largest-ever privacy settlement, for the misuse of location data. It will make a dent, but not a significant one.

The industry as a whole, and particularly the large tech platforms, are clearly in the crosshairs of various governments and legislative bodies.

It behooves every advertiser to support these initiatives, especially when their own trade associations, who represent their interests, are called upon by individual governments to submit information on request. They do, though, act at their own snail-like pace, and while the speed at which governments can act provides guardrails for the industry, this is not always in line with the decisions that you as an advertiser face this quarter.

And advertisers should not be reliant on governments to redress industry imbalance.

Even if and when Google were asked to divest its AdTech business (its exchange, its supply-side technology for publishers, and demand-side platform for buyers) many of the problems of digital advertising would remain. It would maintain leverage in the online ad industry given its dominance in search, browser and consumer data. The AdTech "piping" part of its business generates only a small portion of revenue for the company overall.

It is a part of Google's business, though, that may be just as important to Google as it is in the eyes of regulators. But for different reasons. It enhances Google's other lines of business. It's a trojan horse for captive revenue generation. A one-stop-shop for advertisers to select and transact media, especially useful for advertisers with little media buying expertise.

This synergy between Google's AdTech and media businesses is not always a boon for advertisers. A particular frustration on the buy side is that YouTube inventory can only be transacted through Google's demand-side platform DV360. If an advertiser uses a non-Google DSP to buy CTV ads, they cannot also use it to transact the other main source of video inventory, YouTube. If YouTube agnostically allowed The Trade Desk (TTD) and other DSPs to bid on their inventory, that would be better for everyone.

Selling their own inventory exclusively through their own platforms is a practice that is not unique to Google, but it does become a frustrating bottleneck for buyers. As to whether it's truly monopolistic and anti-competitive, legislators and their vocal constituents will ultimately decide.

Get your hands off my data

Google's AdTech business also gives Google a rich pool of data to make the targeting on its platforms more effective. What is also valuable about its ad network, that doesn't show up in financials, is a huge pipeline of data about who's placing ads and who's getting converted.

While Google will certainly lose out by not having this data, it's not clear if another owner of its ad-tech business would be able to extract the same value,

If the ad network was spun out would anyone be able to benefit as much as Google?

Data access and sharing is the critical component of "interoperability." Negotiations and leverage in the modern digital trading ecosystem are as much about *data access rights* as they are about *fees*.

A clear illustration of how much this can be a detriment to advertiser workstreams, and how little leverage they can have at times, was when Google switched off unfettered access to log-level data from digital trading platforms in 2018. Agencies were used to having access to all manner of signals produced by the trading systems offered by Google. All data that was relevant to a single impression, be that geo data, URLs, cookie IDs, time stamps, viewability measures, and the trading transaction data itself, was a gold mine for agency decision making and agency tools. Overnight, in the run-up to GDPR enforcement in Europe, it was made unavailable by Google. No amount of haggling or extra fee negotiations would budge them. Not even pointing to the fact that most of the data involved was not a privacy concern. In many ways, the privacy legislation that was leading to pressure from statutory authorities was being weaponized by Google to the detriment of advertisers.

Limited access to event-level log data has since been offered by Google to the buy side. Changes to Google's "Ads Data Hub" access on YouTube buys in 2019 were an effective olive branch to the industry.

The buy side, though, remains somewhat hostage to such changes. And data access, and the interoperability across platforms that it affords, is often not apparent.

Most of Facebook's ad dollars don't come from large advertisers. It's surprising and disappointing to observe how many industry observers still think that the threat of a boycott by large advertisers will rattle them in the slightest.

Facebook has 9 million advertisers, according to its own disclosure. The highest-spending 100 of those 9 million brands account for only about 6 percent of the platform's ad revenue (Pathmatics, 2021).

Facebook is primarily a "long tail" business that reaps monies from millions of small and medium-sized businesses. As far as they are concerned this long tail wags the dog.

Even when confronted by large boycotts, the sheer number of advertisers on the platform tends to insulate the company from too much financial fallout. Boycotts may cause more reputational damage than any effects on the bottom line. Plus, they tend to be transient and temporary, given the perceived risks for advertisers from staying off the platform for too long.

The "Great Facebook Boycott of 2020" was a case in point.

That boycott urged companies to stop buying ads on Facebook in July 2020 to protest and bring attention to the platform's handling of hate speech and misinformation. More than 1,000 advertisers publicly joined. Even then, the YOY spend on the platform for the top 100 was only reduced by 12 percent during "peak boycott," with only a few totally dropping all spends. Most were back on within a month.

As Mark Zuckerberg himself said at the time, "Some seem to wrongly assume that our business is dependent on a few large advertisers."

Which all begs the question, if boycotts don't always provide immediate leverage, and if legislative authorities are working on a fixed timeframe, what does effect the most change in behavior amongst the platforms?

Policing each other

The biggest current controllers of the power of each of the platforms tend to be each other. They are in effect influencing each other more than the industry can currently police them. No amount of legislative effort, nor advertiser boycotts, will have the impact that:

1 Apple privacy changes have had on Facebook;

2 cooperation has had on each other;

3 new entrants like Amazon and other retail media platforms have had and will have on the market overall.

The biggest headwind for Facebook's dominance is Apple's privacy policy changes. As a result of Apple's crackdown on in-app tracking and other privacy initiatives on the horizon (Apple's App-Tracking Transparency—ATT—initiative), Meta is in the middle of a long-term reconstruction of its ads business. According to Facebook's own estimates, Apple's changes to their privacy policy cost Facebook $10 billion in 2021 alone. That's because ATT in iOS devices cuts back on tracking by revoking default access to the identifier for advertisers (IDFA)—a unique code that shows when people are seeing an ad on Facebook, googling that product, and buying something via its website, for example.

Apple has not needed to explicitly appease advertisers as much as Facebook or Google, as their primary business isn't funded by advertising. They do, however, all have to worship at the altar of privacy protection, limit sharing of user data with third parties, and operate without cross-app identifiers, including advertising IDs. Like Apple with iOS, Google bear a responsibility to protect the privacy of their Android OS users and are doing so by applying their proposed Privacy Sandbox. But they also want to please advertisers. They are torn between the throes of privacy provision and enabling targeted advertising. And it's that kind of tension that naturally leads to announcements and some delays when it comes to, for example, the demise of third-party cookies, or tried-but-failed attempts to replicate old ways of using data (it will be two years before Android privacy changes, or the total demise of third-party cookie tracking, will come into play).

Most Apple and Google changes in terms of their operating systems are a lose-lose for Facebook. It is questionable whether Facebook's current business model and operations are made for the new era of prioritized privacy, even at a time when privacy has been weaponized. The social media ad boom of the last decade is showing signs of strain. The slowdown is such that the current growth rate is almost in line with traditional media such as linear TV and radio. The growth and appeal of short video format-based platforms like TikTok hasn't helped.

Facebook themselves, though, now openly point to structural changes by other platforms as the prime challenge. They openly accuse Apple of undercutting others in the digital economy… to grow their own business.

There have been industry suspicions that Facebook and Google themselves have at times undercut others for their own benefit. They dispute allegations that, for example, Google held back rivals from using its Open Bidding program and that it rigged ad auctions to favor Facebook (Lomas, 2022). This hasn't stopped investigation of any agreement between Google and Facebook in the European Union and the United Kingdom by antitrust regulators, with claims that it undermined competition in the advertising market.

There are good signs though that ad dollars are demonstrably now shifting towards new types of players. And we increasingly live in an e-commerce-driven landscape. Amazon's own advertising business growth rate is now outpacing others. And other traditional retailers like Walmart and Target have been quietly building digital marketing businesses of their own. They have all learned the central lesson of the commercial history of Google—that having skin in the ad tech tools game (captively) helps their other businesses.

Advertisers clearly have more choice than they used to. These new "retail media" options are also less affected by privacy changes since they do not rely on "third party" datasets or cookies. Critically they have the one piece of leverage that everyone seeks—their own first-party datasets, which they have in common with many advertisers.

Choices for a digital marketer should not just be a menu of technical features. The menu should include various ways of working. "Spray and pray" is a tactic of digital advertising that is most commonly practiced unwittingly, even in the promised land of programmatic precision. Whether using first-party data, third-party data, or no external data outside of the bidstream, the only way to ensure the success of a campaign effort is to have the ability to continually spot-check the quality of what has been delivered, and how it matched with expectations. Without a regular feedback loop based on transparently measured output and equitably quantified input, any proposed changes to the *process* will likely be as fruitful as a slot machine at the Las Vegas airport. When assessing shiny new objects, be those new shops or new data sources, the future impact on a marketer's performance will not be determined by any individual input or process function, but by the way that the feedback system works as a whole for improving output over time. It is vital for marketers to have absolute clarity as to how output is determined, and the explicit levers for input and process that are accessible and within their control.

As we covered in Chapter 5 on the limits of tech, the right attribution methodology is a core principle of measuring any output of an advertising system. The modern marketer should be able to diagram the decision process of how their organization attributes business outcomes to advertising efforts. In a world where the industry jargon around data sources can be as confusing as a foreign language, the simplest way to look at this is tracing whether the "answer" being sought is based on your own information or a supplier's. A marketer that has control of their organization's data will undoubtedly have almost all inputs to their feedback loop based on datasets owned by their organization. If the feedback loop and process of a marketer is based primarily on the data or information of external parties, like the companies selling them the advertising space, this is akin to tautology. Too many marketers operate in a system wherein the negation of particular AdTech efficacy is dependent on the AdTech itself to satisfy; it is close to impossible for technologies to declare themselves ineffective by their own output data and feedback systems.

It has become clear that having your own first-party data, protecting it, developing it, and joining it securely where possible is the path to productivity in today's digital ecosystem.

The inherent leverage of you and your partners

You now have more power than you think. It boils down to a few key things:

- having data
- having frenemies
- having friends and
- having informed free will

First and foremost, there are several unique ways advertisers and their agencies can develop and leverage their first-party datasets.

Some brands are naturally data rich, but for those who aren't it is important to collect it systematically and safely where they can. For the demand side, first-party data might not come as easily as for publishers who have millions of page views flowing through their properties every month, for example. Instead, advertisers need to be a bit more creative about where they source their first-party data.

Among others, advertisers can collect first-party data via website and app analytics, purchase histories, past interactions (email, phone, or in-person logs), social media engagement, email questionnaire and survey responses, pixel/beacon tracking events, or offline systems such as CRM or mailing lists.

For brands that might not have a regular flow of website visitors, such as CPG brands, the challenge is a bit more robust. In these cases, advertisers might use techniques such as micro-sites, real-world experiences, or launch

D2C initiatives to engage more directly with customers. It's worth noting that leveraging first-party data for advertising cannot match the scale of third-party cookies, because you can only target users who've already engaged with you. That said, the accuracy of third-party audiences can be a bit underwhelming when examined, so you can at least rest assured that your targeting will be far more accurate. The obvious downsides of only targeting users that exist in your first-party datasets and intend to spend the full budget, include but are not limited to: being limited to addressing the consumer device used for a single interaction; significant increase in exposure frequency levels; widening the array of media selection beyond known relationships; and paying a price per impression that is significantly higher than the market.

Acknowledging the underwhelming accuracy of third-party datasets for consumer demographics and intent, it is healthy for a marketer to implement controls according to the targeting and bidding being "spray and pray" in practice. Controlling the direction and the level of spray while leaning on measurement more than prayer is what the successful marketer of the modern digital world must excel at. Without minimizing the daunting nature of this work in an environment of frenemies, marketers must remember that there is not only beauty in simplicity, but also operational efficiency. If your inputs and outputs are not clearly and simply defined in the same taxonomy, the process decisions will always seem like a gamble that cannot be predictably tuned.

The first step in making data valuable in action is to ensure it is structured and labeled according to the needs and design of your process. Common taxonomy, congruent data structures, and reliable cadences of event streams should not just be the deferred dreams expressed at engineering stand-up meetings, but should be the first port of call of any senior marketer. A marketer that knows the rules of the game is positioned well, but pointless if they don't know exactly what pieces are theirs to use. If you have a six-sided die, and your peers are using dice with 10 sides, you'll be playing very different games over the course of time.

For those marketers not formally trained or educated in the bits and bytes, modern nuts and bolts, of ad technologies, you can think of big data as a supercharged spreadsheet that is too heavy for a tiny engine like your standard software to operate. These large databases of advertising events with 24 column headers and 24 billion rows of entries require heavy machinery in the form of cloud computing, a bigger computer somewhere else. Similar to how you can carry a small stone but need a crane to move a boulder.

Unfortunately, marketing has not always taken kindly to the limitations and laws of physics, often incentivized to look beyond in an aspirational vision.

The congruence of taxonomy can be written off as a nice-to-have by marketers who might not intend to stick around long enough to be assessed by the results they deliver. In reality, it is the most essential foundation in a marketer's approach to avoid confusion, unseen mishaps, and unmeasured waste. The format, structure, and language of the sites or apps you wish to target must be the same as the reports received detailing where all the ads were served. If you wish to target "abc.com" and "com. FunGameApp", to have an efficient measurement system, your delivery reports cannot be accepted as "http://abc.com/sf/mobile/24398cs7sd.html" or "com.FGA23988233423app.ios" respectively. There is less dexterity in the big data world, similar to how you can brush dirt off a stone while carrying it, but a crane cannot do the same to a boulder. Correcting the formatting of data output is manageable at a small scale, but can disrupt and impede all analysis processes if required at the scale of billions or even hundreds of millions of data records. This prerequisite of congruency applies not only to domains, but to datapoints like timestamps, user agents, platform identifiers, supply chain parties, creative asset identifiers, IP addresses, geographic regions, device types, and more.

Once your data is in place, there is a basic playbook associated with getting the most out of it, as illustrated below:

- **Using your own data to build profiles and identifiers**
  In order for your dataset to have utility for online advertising, it often has to be used with tools that transform the data into usable digital formats. Offline segments or customer profiles have to be able to translate to an online targetable session on a mobile, PC, or other device. All of which has to be managed in a manner in line with privacy requirements around PII (personally identifiable information). "Hashing" (or transforming of data into simple anonymous character strings) is the go-to technique that facilitates the safe cleansing and matching of datasets. Email datasets, for example, can be hashed and augmented with other datasets, making them targetable on the open web. There are already many competing universal IDs, frameworks that enable inferred device and ID retargeting, and targeting that can be enabled through cohorts or segments modeled from an advertiser's first-party data—with more in the pipeline. Any advertiser in the programmatic ecosystem will need to choose, integrate with, and test at least a few of these IDs to discover which will work best to achieve their particular goals. Try to ensure that the most valuable part of this equation is the data that you own and provide yourself.

- Using "data clean rooms" for secure matching with other datasets

  The concept of the data clean room isn't necessarily new, but it's one that's coming into its own as we lurch toward a future without cookies. Data clean rooms are like escrow for digital advertising; they provide a secure environment where advertisers can anonymously share their first-party data with trusted partners, including both walled gardens (Google, Facebook) and third-party partners. They can do this without directly exposing any of their data or entering into any data-sharing agreements. Think of the clean room like a secure vault: once inside, any PII is hashed, meaning it can't be pulled by any other party. Clean room technology can carry out secure first-party data matching in a few different ways:

  i. Matching your own anonymized first-party data with the ad performance data of the partner in question (e.g., a Google campaign). For example, you may discover that a particular creative coincided with a sale at a particular moment, then use that insight to further tweak a campaign.

  ii. Matching your own first-party audience with the publisher's first-party audience on the sell side. Once matched, advertisers can leverage private deals built by the publisher to target supply from matched users.

  iii. Matching first-party datasets with other available datasets to augment levels of insight and/or redefine existing segments. You may already have plenty of information about these users, but matching in this way can enrich the data with even more valuable data points.

- Using your own data to replace increasingly defunct cookie-retargeting methods

  As discussed, cookies are on their way out. As a tracking method they are out of sync with growing privacy demands. They have also, arguably, been useless as a viable method of "retargeting." Retargeting has traditionally been one of the most popular forms of digital advertising, and it basically involves offering a second chance to engage with prospects off-property. Finding them elsewhere on the web, basically. Which of course is creepy. Hence the privacy issue. Advertisers should already be beginning to phase out any reliance on third-party solutions for running retargeting campaigns—but it is still possible to do it using their own first-party data. To do so at scale, advertisers will need to rely either on the data clean room approach discussed above or rely on one of the universal ID solutions being developed across the industry.

- **Using your own data to replace increasingly defunct new customer prospecting methods based on "lookalike" audiences**
  The core assumption here is that people with similar "attributes" are likely to make similar purchases as known customers. Using available datasets to identify those attributes and finding evidence of them online is key. The second part of that statement (finding them online) has traditionally relied somewhat on cookies. Now that they are being phased out, we must adopt different methods that further rely on owned datasets. For example, you might want to focus on those customers who spend more on your site, visit more frequently, or simply convert more often. You can then peek into the bidstream and identify what you know about them—device type, operating system, browser language, geo-location, etc.—and combine that data with any third-party sources, like age and gender, or other more potent indicators.

  If you're not seeing the results you want, you can shift your parameters, update your lookalikes, and try again. Of course, at least for now, this side of the equation still relies on third-party cookies, but it's safe to assume that cookie-less solutions (likely those powered by universal IDs) won't take long to hit the market once cookies go away.

- **Using your own data to improve outcomes**
  Your first-party data can be used to tweak your creative strategy based on first-party insights via dynamic creative optimization (DCO). For example, you might use your visitor's on-site activity to deploy creatives that specifically target users who have taken specific actions (for example, added a product to their basket but never checked out), or serve ads dynamically based on a user's attributes (for example, showing platinum credit cards to specific visitors based on income bracket). Or users who have engaged with content about specific products or services, but never booked a demo. By enriching your own audiences in this way, you can reduce time-to-value for customers actively engaging with your brand. You can also use these creative strategies to discover what works on which type of user, then adjust your strategy to generate creatives that convert more customers

All of the above are reflective of a world of data enrichment—basically one of adding value to existing datasets. The difference between before and after the advent of the era of privacy is that you, as a data owner of first-party datasets, have an extremely important asset at your disposal. As the months tick by until the loss of third-party cookies, you should focus on the strategies mentioned above to start building a silo of proprietary data. Of course, the industry is working on multiple third-party identity solutions to replace the cookie—but it stands you in good stead to prepare sooner rather than later.

Perhaps the biggest casualty of the cookiepocalypse will be the loss of measurement accuracy and ROI calculation, as well as a reduction in addressability at scale. With the reliance (or perhaps overreliance) on third-party audiences from data providers and buying platforms, advertisers have become comfortable being able to address enormous audiences. The only problem is that, even at their very best, third-party audiences were always a little questionable in terms of accuracy. (One study found that 84 percent of users within a certain third-party segment were identified as *both* male and female.) So, in reality, while the loss of the third-party cookie will still impact measurement and ROI calculation, its effect on addressability might not be as severe as we anticipate. In fact, thanks to the deterministic nature of first-party data, targeting might actually *improve*, but at the cost of scale. While the industry knocks heads together to agree on an identity solution, the best thing advertisers can do is begin building their first-party data silos and learning how best to activate them.

That's what you can do alone. What about in conjunction with others?

Friends and frenemies

Advertisers always like to follow what other advertisers do.

They are always interested in peer-to-peer comparisons with like-minded competitors. It's an industry of nosey neighbors and copycats. Some of the best campaigns are works of "homage" so to speak. As the saying goes, "talent imitates, genius steals."

But what about when it comes to working together to fight the multiple headwinds in today's digital industry? Just how effective are joint industry efforts in tackling the issues of transparency, for example?

Advertisers have national and global industry associations working on their behalf. The World Federation of Advertisers (WFA), the Association of National Advertisers (ANA), and the Incorporated Society of British Advertisers (ISBA) are some of many. The Interactive Advertiser Bureau (IAB) likely has the widest impact, spanning globally and having a membership that is made up of publishers, advertisers, and every business in between. They all aim to represent the interests of their members

They are also open to regular critiques from the sidelines. Some of those critiques verge on the conspiratorial, almost as if adland has its own version of Q-Anon. But given the scale and nature of the issues that the industry faces, this can only be expected.

It is easy to be churlish about industry bodies, and it doesn't always help. What does help is to support the growing number of cross-advertiser and cross-industry initiatives that are addressing them head-on.

There is nothing wrong with advertisers joining forces to address transparency issues; in many ways, that is the most impactful way that they can.

The very fact that there are multiple ongoing governmental and statutory authorities investigating the industry is indicative of the fact that the ad industry has failed to self-regulate. Ongoing cross-industry cooperative efforts, whilst noble, tend to be (i) late, (ii) time-consuming, and (iii) mired by the intricacies of the AdTech landscape.

It took two years to complete ISBA's investigation for their transparency report in 2020. And ongoing investigations, such as the ANA's, are reportedly ladened with data access complications (Shields, 2022).

What they do achieve, without a doubt, is a pushing of the envelope in terms of what can and cannot be accomplished with available datasets. Plus, they are good at exposing the degree and willingness to participate of all parties in the programmatic ecosystem.

Making informed choices

Transparency should not be an "ask." It should be a given. Complete visibility and monitoring are foundational governance associated with any digital buy.

The very fact that any media platform or content partner is not willing to be transparent should in and of itself be part of your assessment of them as partners. If someone is not willing to share the digital records of what you pay for or is reticent about the use of your preferred independent tracker, you can always do the one thing that is open to all advertisers—you can walk away.

As we will cover in our last chapter, for advertisers, pumping ad dollars into a media company or a tech platform is an investment with an inherent risk profile. There is always a downside as well as an upside that is usually demonstrable.

Advertisers can leave any platform when that perceived downside outweighs any perceived benefit. The threat of vacating your financial presence on a platform is always a better piece of leverage than a temporary boycott.

Getting the best possible outcome for your needs involves using everything at your disposal: your data-wielding friends and frenemies, ideally making complex decisions easier, based on the right tools and processes available. It's about having tools you can trust, which often let the data do the talking for you. Tools with teeth.

In any negotiation, or in the case of a bad partner, a dispute, it's the granularity and simplicity of the evidence that often counts. It's difficult for example, to claim for invalid traffic with a publisher whilst referencing aggregated general datasets. The more granular the data, the more it cannot be argued with, the better.

If you have a good "supply path mapping" workstream in place, as outlined in Chapter 2, then more often than not, the data can do the talking for you.

It is ideal if the tools you deploy (i) have maximum coverage of all ad events, and (ii) are "deterministic" in their nature. By deterministic, we mean that there are no hidden workings for the technique involved, and the outputs of the measures are simple and clear for all to see. If your measurement includes some hidden magic, "machine learning," or any probabilistic modeling, then their power for *negotiation purposes* with media owners or platforms is minimized.

The great barrier of grief

Sometimes having simple and deterministic evidence is not enough. Even if you have all the granular evidence in the world that you need, and that evidence is apparent and definitive to all. In many ways the industry can work in byzantine ways where a definitive truth offered up in a simple dataset is not enough.

One of the main areas where this is most apparent is when trying to reclaim monies or "claw-backs" from media partners and platforms.

As we outlined earlier, the money in adland flows with a force in one direction, while volume-based billing incentives are a force in the opposite direction. If budgets are being spent and money is flowing then media owners, tech platforms, and agencies are all happy because they are all making money.

The "fun" starts when a dataset from a buyer deterministically asks for a monetary "claw-back." That's often when an immovable object meets an irresistible force. The systems and structures in adland are not always made for that kind of ask.

When it comes to ad fraud, many platforms offer refunds, but only on their terms. They can claim that the inventory in question is fraud-free based on their own measures. The only problem is that it tends to be their own proprietary (i.e. secret) determination with either (i) no third-party measurement player involved and/or (ii) cursory references to an existing verification software that is an "approved partner." On the publisher side, everyone is free to participate in self-declared initiatives from the likes of the "Trustworthy Accountability Group" (TAG, 2022), which some say is better than nothing, but others claim is doing the industry a disservice.

There is no independent "referee" in a marketplace where different verification companies supply different and competing measures to both the buy side and the sell side of the industry. And where Google and Facebook mark their own homework.

There are also some other factors at play that can complicate an advertiser's ability to gain monetary claw-backs or at least credits:

- the financial and legal aspects of any claw-back can get messy if it involves advertisers, agencies, an agency trading partner, a DSP, SSPs/exchanges, and publishers;

- contractual clauses have to be in place that specifically refer to and support these eventualities and make specific reference to who is accountable;

- partners may provide upfront options to buy only from exchanges that will refund media spend for fraudulent inventory, but again the definitions of fraudulent can be opaque.

Perhaps the most frustrating aspect of it is working through the system with your "rep" from a media supplier. Often, they don't know who to ask or can be defensive as well as deflective in their approach to a resolution. Brushing the issue under the rug and a templatized apology is unfortunately sufficient in most cases. And they are, as one anonymous industry veteran said, "not always proactively engaged or even interested in our campaign's success." Like a river flowing from a mountain of ice melt, as long as the advertising money flows, there will be no riots downstream. The ideal situation would be that the same pressure can be exerted in pursuit of transparency in the other direction. A financial riot or boycott by marketers is undoubtedly more impactful than a fit thrown by a supplier.

Claw-backs are totally achievable though. Many advertisers have added language to media contracts stating they will not pay for invalid traffic, and that the definition of invalid traffic should be made explicit and the source of that truth clear. In effect, they state upfront that unless a partner works with a given agreed source of truth, then they will vote with their feet.

Having *informed free will* is your ultimate leverage.

References

Brin, S and Page, L (1998) The anatomy of a large-scale hypertextual web search engine, *Computer Networks and ISD Systems*, 30 (1–7), pp 107–17 https://www.sciencedirect.com/science/article/abs/pii/S016975529800110X (archived at https://perma.cc/P2F6-SGUC)

Brereton, D (2022) Google Search is dying, *DKB*, https://dkb.io/post/google-search-is-dying (archived at https://perma.cc/6634-ZK4B)

eBiquity (2022) Google, Meta and Amazon are on track to absorb more than 50% of all ad money in 2022, https://www.ebiquity.com/news-insights/press/google-meta-and-amazon-are-on-track-to-absorb-more-than-50-of-all-ad-money-in-2022/ (archived at https://perma.cc/3S7X-B3G3)

Lomas, N (2022) 'Jedi Blue' ad deal between Google and Facebook sparks new antitrust probes, *TechCrunch*, https://techcrunch.com/2022/03/11/google-meta-jedi-blue-eu-uk-antitrust-probes/ (archived at https://perma.cc/Q8GT-NG87)

Pathmatics (2021) Facebook Ad Intelligence 2021, https://www.pathmatics.com/facebook (archived at https://perma.cc/P4GT-PATQ)

Shields, R (2022) The ANA's transparency crackdown has been mired by ad tech's intricacies, *Digiday*, https://digiday.com/marketing/the-anas-transparency-crackdown-has-been-mired-by-ad-techs-intricacies/ (archived at https://perma.cc/HK3S-LB86)

TAG (2022) TAG Certified Against Fraud Program, https://www.tagtoday.net/certifications (archived at https://perma.cc/4TUN-5X6S)

Zippia (2022) Zippia Advertising Statistics, https://www.zippia.com/advice/advertising-statistics/ (archived at https://perma.cc/7HHW-CLS5)

Risks versus rewards

Making decisions in media buying was once a very human concern. The scale of decision making was manageable without too many heavy complications. How should I set my budget? What's my scheduling and flighting strategy? Burst, pulse, or drip? Across how many channels? Topping and tailing? What kind of syndicated programming? At what effective frequency?

All of which were standard questions, most of them answerable with reference to manageable datasets, a handy spreadsheet, or a bit of clever analysis. The extent to which technology was involved in that decision making was relatively limited.

Buyers were a certain breed. "Gorillas with calculators" as the saying went. Not necessarily tech savvy. Because they didn't need to be. More Gordon Gekko than geek.

Still human of course, within reason. With attitudes towards risk taking pretty much in line with what you would expect from individuals within a company setting, spending other people's money, with personal incentives typically aligned with salaries and bonuses linked to client measures of success, if they were lucky. Typical practice was being obsessed with avoiding perceived losses and maximizing perceived gains.

No one got fired for recommending and subsequently booking media for a 30-second TV spot, with target deliveries of 400 ratings per month, and an effective frequency target of 3+ exposures. In the same way that no one tends to get fired now by recommending Google and Facebook.

Not yet anyway.

Place your bets

As there are some signs that big tech's era of invincibility could be over. While Google retains knowledge of our shopping baskets and internet search terms, Facebook and some others have shown their limitations, with a dependency on personal data that's vulnerable to regulation and public opinion. And a palpable sense of distrust from advertisers over a lack of transparency and increased competition for attention from newcomer TikTok have also loosened their grip.

There were some signs at the back end of 2022 when the giants of Silicon Valley started going through some serious shrinkage. Facebook laid off up to 15 percent of its workforce, Twitter half, Snap 20 percent. The combined revenues of the largest tech companies, Alphabet (Google), Amazon, Apple, Meta (Facebook), and Microsoft, soared during the 2020–2021 pandemic (19 percent then 28 percent growth). They are now back to 2019 pre-pandemic levels. Some of their travails are down to hiring binges and general mismanagement. And the jury is still out on whether the $18 billion spent by Meta on the "metaverse" whilst the largest source of revenue via ads for them is on Facebook, counts as the largest bad bet of all time. But this does also reflect how they are being challenged by some of the very same "horses of the ad apocalypse" we outlined in the introduction:

1 new competitors eating their lunch (TikTok biting at Facebook, Netflix, and Apple ad offerings);

2 having too much asymmetrical power (calls for the breakup of Google, Apple flexing its privacy muscles making space for itself in the ad game);

3 industry associations calling foul on opaque audience supply chains (ongoing investigations);

4 regulatory and privacy authorities sharpening their axes (both in terms of privacy and monopolistic practices).

For the best part of the last decade, YouTube has fulfilled its role as the "TV option online" for many consumer goods brands. It continues to attract spending but, perhaps critically, at the end of 2022 Google reported that YouTube ad revenue was down for the first time.

So new bets are being considered by ad buyers. Assessments being made.

Advanced TV/CTV, retail media, and gaming/esports are three of the current "causes du jour" among advertisers looking to increase spends (Waters, 2022). As we have seen, not all of them are transparent and measurable. Changes in "betting patterns" in digital advertising aren't always uniform or logical. Advertisers at times will prioritize search advertising and cut back on the kind of display ads that populate Facebook feeds (Joseph, 2022). Which is indicative of longer-term issues being thrust to the surface, short-term performance demands, and advertisers acting accordingly to maintain returns where possible. They are an expedient bunch. And their media buyers are averse not only to any loss of ROI, but also "loss of face."

Loss aversions

The granddaddy of decision-making psychology, Dan Kahneman, was once invited to present in front of an enthralled audience of ad agency execs (IPA, 2014).

He is like Elvis for adland planning geeks. He reminded an enthralled audience that we all have a "limited capacity for effort." Which was of course generally not news for a lot of the agency folks in attendance, whose productivity can come in bursts and drips. But it was specifically a useful reminder that ad execs were just as prone to faulty decision making as everyone else. Prone to biases. Influenced by perceived norms. Taking the paths of least resistance. With aversions to perceived loss.

As he quoted from his book *Thinking, Fast and Slow*, "We are blind to our blindness." We tend to see what we are motivated to see. We like rules of thumb. Handy guidelines. And we are averse to registering perceived losses.

As a result, the advertising industry can be full of dangerous micro-delusions that are born of us convincing ourselves that a given option is correct, a given measure is good, a given outcome "in line with expectations." And that it's conventional wisdom. For example, we have somewhat deluded ourselves that "impressions" is a potent currency, when it might just be a machine-to-machine process.

The overarching promise of digital has been to minimize such faulty human reasoning and facilitate campaign deployment and feedback at a scale that humans cannot grasp. And of course, machines have traditionally performed well with things that involve a given set of tasks, with clear parameters and fixed goals.

Digital media buying has offered the one thing that would enable minimized risk taking and promote "fully informed decision making"—accurate feedback loops and seamless actions.

How machines influence risk taking

Research has shown that robots can encourage people to take greater risks in a simulated gambling scenario than they would if there was nothing to influence their behaviors (Hanoch, 2021).

In the same way that peer pressure can lead us all to riskier behaviors, apparently having a machine as an assistant can also have some unintended consequences. It makes sense because it represents a scenario where we have outsourced some of our responsibilities and hence some of our "loss of face" risks.

"It wasn't me. A big machine did it and ran away."

Imagine a situation where media buyers do not have to risk losing face because they can point to a world where algorithmic buying makes dynamic decisions, and third-party verification technology is in place. Any bots are being ticked as good bots. Bots are trading with bots, and the feedback they provide is "accurate." That is the fantasy world that many in the industry are currently being asked to live in.

And of course, the machinery itself can mask the degree of risk involved. The decisions that are being made in programmatic buying are largely invisible to the buyer. Many advertisers are blind to the inner workings of even the most popular platforms and buying tools. Their proponents can obfuscate and deflect and point to the one thing they know will appeal— demonstrable efficiencies or improved outcomes.

It's beyond imperative therefore that the methods involved are indeed accurate—in the data involved in feedback, and the associated financials in the trades involved.

Leaving Las Vegas

On the content side, many media owners and platforms have seen and exploited cheap avenues to growth through questionable practices that have seen lax policies on content moderation and content monetization. A future of unchecked and un-curated machine-on-machine content creation and ad optimization in this context is pure madness. It will lead to brands being exposed to horrific contexts and appearing in unknown or unfiltered areas. The brand safety risks are now too great. When trying to assess the safety of your brand in the context of any content or media platform based on user contributions, we must start by looking at who is posting rather than what they are posting. The ease of anonymity of the user can be directly correlated to the degree of vile or inflammatory discourse on that platform. Meaning that a user-generated content or social media platform will have fewer brand safety risks because of contextual flags if the users are validated, authenticated, and disclosed. It is no surprise that web forums like

4chan, 8chan, and other cesspools of atrocious human thinking are centered around anonymity and have user bases full of "anons." Many ad-supported media platforms, referred to as social networks for the public, are in transition periods and working through their corporate coming-of-age stories. Not all will come out on the other side in a state that is familiar or recognizable to all of us bystanders and participants, but this metamorphosis is natural and necessary.

And on the buy side, as we have also outlined, the way the trading ecosystem itself works is often murky in its current form. There has been a lot of interest in the past few years about transparency in the supply path. After reading most of the commentary and headlines about "the unaccountable 15 percent" of monies that could not be traced in the 2020 ISBA study referenced in Chapter 2, or the "50 percent of monies that never get anywhere near publishers," it's easy to start equating the ecosystem with gambling and gaming devices.

Everyone will be familiar with slot machines. The largest traditional ones are the size of a fridge, with some proper old-school electromechanics. The latest ones are fully computerized. People queue up to try them, like new clients seduced by a new tech in town.

Some have a great return on spend, but most lose money. They have no control in that regard, and of course that can sometimes be part of the fun in any gamble.

The owners of the devices and the casinos do have control. They own any magic money boxes that store all the machine's takings, and everyone else's losses. They have complete visibility on the bit that matters to them—the path from your budgets to the magic money box that only they have access to. They themselves have no interest in the underlying mechanics, as long as there is money in the take box. And they have no interest in knowing exactly how much you have spent or lost, as long as you are spending. As long as the machine is busy.

The more you play, the more they win. Getting you to play is their core incentive. Better still, they don't have any obligation to declare their take to anyone. No auditors. No commercial or moral contract in sight.

Of course, this is not directly analogous to the state of transparency in the digital supply path, as contracts, auditors, and verification specialists exist. But how many incentives exist, are they aligned, is there only one magic money box, how many keys are there, and who has them?

There is a pervasive underlying fear in adland that (i) dollars are poured into areas of the media mix that are, in many ways, unaccountable and wasted, and (ii) this is connected to apparent declines in overall ad effectiveness.

There is some evidence that declines in effectiveness have coincided with the rise in digital, but that evidence is not definitive, and the debate is still ongoing as to whether there is a "crisis of effectiveness."

But the prospect alone is spurring senior marketers to reorganize their teams and find partners that actually help change this dynamic and attempt to categorically improve the outcome of their spending. This is truer for large advertisers than small and medium-sized ones, who are still prone to the currently pervasive sentiment that everything starts and ends with using Google or Facebook.

But new playbooks are emerging. The question is whether they will have to be updated continuously. There is a "tyranny of nowness" as we seem to lurch from one platform change to another, from one privacy mandate to another, from one crisis to another.

The transparency playbook

Throughout this book we have already touched upon different elements of this new constantly evolving playbook. It involves:

1 making sure your data is a strategic and tactical asset;

2 determining what parts of digital operations you can/can't own;

3 future-proofing your tech stack and partnerships;

4 minimizing your reliance on other people's measurement or optimizations.

For all of you that have skipped to the back of the book for a summary of recommendations, you are in luck. We get it, you are busy. And we have worked long enough in the industry to know that a handy to-do list is very welcome. It remains an industry full of time-pressed, overworked people.

So here is a list of the "what" to dos.

But don't do anything blindly. There is enough of that going on in adland already. To understand the "hows" and "whys" you are going to have to reach the appropriate chapter.

Some of this you can do on your own, some of it is dependent on healthy and transparent partnerships.

The era of privacy, and the shift towards opt-in first-party data-based advertising, opens the door for advertisers. Brands reduce their reliance on

Table 8.1   Top ten issues and recommendations

Issue	Recommendation
Advertiser-side, there is a **capability skills gap**, particularly in the areas of digital transparency and measurement.	Lean in. Treat agency and tech partners as sources of platform knowledge and training as well as executional partners.
There are ongoing **persistent trust issues** in the industry, particularly in programmatic trading.	Critically, learn from peers. Arguably, as an advertiser, you are the only one truly on the demand side, and trade associations that try to represent those interests, and third parties with no skin in the game, should be fully engaged.
The era of privacy has meant that a number of practices around the **use of data can be toxic**.	Develop, own, protect and leverage your own first-party datasets. Reduce the degree of reliance on increasingly defunct and depreciated sources.
Many of these issues help fuel **a temptation to in-house** media planning and buying capability.	Determine whether your business is currently in-house friendly, in terms of data and tech access, and in terms of the cadence and type of media you buy. Resource plan. Decide what executional capabilities you want to own. If none, at least own your own strategy. If some, set clear KPIs.
The industry currently operates with **multiple misaligned incentives**. Agency and tech partners' behaviors are not always aligned with your own goals.	Partner selection is no longer a "single tier" issue. Make sure that your partner diligence also reflects the suppliers that sit behind the partner capabilities you are investing in.
Digital trading partners have to be **actively managed** if not policed.	Manage your partners well. Not only via foundational contracts, with clearly stated requirements on things like data shares and fraud rebates, but also, critically, in a manner that fosters good daily behaviors, particularly with agencies. Cut down the number of exchange partners used where possible.

(continued)

Table 8.1 (Continued)

Issue	Recommendation
Some **measurement practices** in digital practice rarely get beyond "vanity metrics" and box-ticking tasks.	Measure what matters, and connect it to clear goals. Use independent third-party sources where possible. Avoid vanity metrics and, critically, give measurement an operational utility. Owning the use of digital verification technology is critical.
Third-party **policies around data shares and access** are sometimes counter-productive to transparency efforts.	Augment existing measurement approaches in areas where your partners are not always incentivized to help. Contractually supported log-level data access, and the use of supply path mapping methods, are two good examples.
There is often **limited independent accountability with new platforms** and channels. Tags that work on one platform may not work on others.	Adapt existing approaches to transparency to new options where possible. Work with partners that can overcome the challenges posed by any walled gardens or new formats like CTV.
Operational **ways of working** are not always in line with the new landscape and partnerships required.	Adapt, repeat and make daily habits of the behaviors associated with each of the things outlined above.

other people's optimizations by linking their own first-party datasets to privacy-friendly other aggregate ones. Tech behemoth changes (like Apple's iOS updates) will only accelerate the need for this.

Making friends and developing partnerships is key though. These partners can be thought of as either "independent friends" and/or "dependent frenemies." There are an increasing number of different organizations involved in the planning and buying supply chain, all with their own commercial interests, which are not always aligned with the interests of the client.

Advertisers need to be sure that they have received the best independent advice that delivers on the transparency promises of their relationship and contracts, primarily for transparency in the financial supply chain. For the data supply chain, they can do a lot themselves plus lean into industry initiatives.

Closed feedback loops

Transparency and control over the underlying technologies that power the industry is not always in the hands of all advertisers. Nor is it always in their agent's grasp.

For all the multitude of ways in which a brand can connect with consumers there is a disconnect. Many brands don't have direct relationships with their consumer base. They are dependent on intermediaries and their datasets. Publishers, technology platforms and, somewhat perennially, retailers.

And the modern retailers of the digital ecosystem who have a real grasp on what works and what doesn't are the ones who have their own "closed feedback loops."

Amazon has its own ad delivery technology, and its own walled garden of users. So do Google and Facebook, but Amazon also has a closed loop of attribution to commercial transactions. They are literally copying the platform playbooks of old, and then adding some. It is no accident that they are currently experiencing YOY double-digit growth in attracting ad spend. The retail media market is projected to grow to $100 billion in the next five years, and to account for 25 percent of all digital spend by 2026 (Wiener et al, 2022). Spending by advertisers on retailers' owned channels will grow at a rate of 22 percent per year over the next five years. It will reshape the media landscape, as well as the retail landscape.

On paper, control and transparency can be significantly better in retail media businesses than in traditional approaches. This advantage enables brands to measure and monitor performance closely and to adjust spending allocations in channels. The benefits are so great for marketers under pressure to demonstrate returns. They can certainly help close the loop on immediate short-term response and sales effectiveness.

They potentially also have what marketers refer to as "full-funnel" capability. Reach is of course key for brand building, and first-party, exclusive inventory helps with both incremental reach and more holistic frequency controls (i.e. when buying third-party media). And the e-commerce insights that these platforms have are key for performance marketing, but they can also support audience and channel strategies by informing media planning, buying, and optimization.

But remember, some of the largest retail media players have a rocky history of sharing datasets for any "greater good." The EU has accused Amazon of "systematically" using data from its marketplace that others can't get (EU Commission, 2020).

Plus, there is no guarantee that use of these retail media company trading platforms ensures unfettered brand safety and invalid traffic controls.

We know from our own supply path mapping work that certain companies regularly refuse access to trading logs to supplement independent measurement workstreams. Agencies are often disintermediated as a result, and at the mercy of the technology partners they work with.

There is a "technology deficit" in parts of adland—and brands and agencies are in a constant battle to ensure they are not left behind. Skilling up is a constant task.

The marketing budgets of the largest advertisers are constantly under pressure. As we face a few years of recession, the majority of budget gatekeepers say their budgets will decrease overall, but key digital and performance-focused channels will increase (WFA, 2022). Retail media is not surprisingly the number one channel in terms of growth. They are taking spending from other digital channels as well as traditional non-digital ones. There's some sentiment amongst the marketing community that the effectiveness of Google and Facebook doesn't necessarily "warrant the spend" (Waters, 2022).

A combination of Apple's ATT moves and the rise of TikTok among advertiser-friendly younger cohorts has led brands to significantly reconsider investment in Facebook. The number of advertisers expecting to increase or decrease their spends on Facebook "next year" used to be 54 percent (increase) versus 8 percent (decrease). Those same figures are now 23 percent (increase) versus 30 percent (decrease). TikTok has a +72 percent net investment sentiment among advertisers (WARC, 2022).

TikTok is clearly disrupting social media options. It is currently the leader in the use of providing content feeds based on interests, not based on who you follow. Instagram and Twitter are now beginning to copy this as it is a critical component of why the overall TikTok experience is winning.

TikTok is also changing the degree of reliance on traditional search. Not only can you search on the platform itself, but critically there is less need for traditional search *the more you are being fed relevant content*. Younger consumers are not doing as much traditional search, according to Google themselves (Dentsu, 2022).

Of course, Amazon also drives people away from traditional search behaviors in a comparable manner. These new algorithmically driven content platforms combined with retail media offerings are what the big incumbents fear most.

Retailers are launching media networks because it drives conversions to their core businesses. It also leverages the datasets at their fingertips. Cast iron clarities on privacy compliance requirements for the industry are a prerequisite for this (an area where some countries and authorities are still lax), the emergent patchwork confusion in the US itself being a case in point (Boyle, 2022).

But these retailer and e-commerce-based datasets are key for another reason. Since the very beginning of the digital era, advertisers have been sold a dream of precision. They have been told that "personalization" was where it was at. As we have outlined earlier, there is no evidence that (i) this works or (ii) has actually been achieved, and the most basic of identifiers such as IP address can be inaccurate, spoofed, or when used go very wrong for someone living in the wrong place at the wrong time.

There is a difference between something being personalized and something feeling personally relevant (the former by definition doesn't include other people—the latter can). Something can feel personal to you *but also to millions of other people*. That is how advertising has always worked.

In many ways, retail media datasets will be able to take advantage of this—use available datasets that are not necessarily personal identifiers, and determine what might feel relevant to you at this time at this place. Relevancy can be achieved without sacrificing privacies. They also have established and longstanding ways of working with brands directly. Plus, some have established ways of managing and augmenting datasets. Disintermediation of agencies in adland may have found a new avenue.

The only problem is that similar things were said about Google and Facebook at one time, and we may just be on the verge of replacing one medieval fiefdom with others. And ads on Amazon might not win any industry prizes, yet.

New fiefdoms

In many ways we are entering a period of new offerings. New options for advertisers beyond (i) simply buying the usual suspect behemoths, and/or (ii) navigating their way through the open web with a patchwork quilt of partnerships.

The growth of retail media partners is giving advertisers pause when it comes to simply repeating annual plans.

And the launch of Netflix's own AdTech business is proving to be a case in point, where advertisers are assessing whether being asked to pay a premium for audience access, whilst being promised reassurances on transparency, is enough. The company is keen to entice advertisers to the new platform with declared brand safety measures and transparencies, involving not only digital verification partners, but also national ratings panel providers in the UK and US (BARB, 2022).

On top of this, the quieter, hidden side of Apple that is focused on advertising is getting bigger. And there is every indication that it is building a self-service platform for businesses to book ads to be served to customers through Apple products (Shields, 2022).

These are all developments that advertisers of course welcome and, subject to the normal diligence and checks on promised transparencies, support.

Beyond these new walls, the "Open Web" represents the multitude of mid-tail and long-tail publishers not controlled by the large walled gardens of Google, Facebook, and Amazon. This is also one area that is involving new types of partnerships that advertisers should be more aware of and ask questions about:

- DSPs are making stronger connections with publisher inventories. These new offerings allow advertisers on given DSPs to bid directly on publisher inventory without the typical SSP/exchange involvement. These arrangements tend to involve large publishers. It is a move that on the surface looks like a bypassing of SSPs.

- Meanwhile, agencies have been striking deals with SSPs, often under the banner of "supply path optimization," which on the surface of it bypasses and irritates DSPs.

These trends are largely a result of the advent of header bidding and the rise in importance of understanding the digital supply path. Header bidding enables publishers to solicit bids from as many sources as possible and have them compete in a holistic auction that the publisher controls. SSPs and exchanges have become commodities that play in an open and democratized bid stream. They are still good at aggregating demand from a bunch of DSPs, but if a DSP is large enough it can make more sense for them to connect with publishers directly.

When it comes to bidding on the open web, beyond the confines of the established and newer walled gardens, not all advertisers are aware of these arrangements. But they have to be. Especially when it comes to claimed optimizations.

Advertisers should be asking some questions about these arrangements. How is deciding to throw money at a particular exchange "SPO"? What is the nature of these agreements? Are they cost based, and what does the cost/quality trade-off look like? Will they be better than actively using available datasets in the context of agency optimization tools that are much touted and pitched but sometimes less heard of afterwards? And how do they compare with the efforts of DSPs (e.g. TTD's Open Path project launched in 2022) themselves making connections with publishers?

Digital is "having a moment"

Advertising investment has always had elements of risk. The gambits of the past were made and mitigated based on an understanding of (i) the mechanics of trading and (ii) the lay of the land in terms of relationships between suppliers. And now it is no different. To approach both the closed and open web properly demands new skillsets, new levels of awareness, and a patchwork quilt of partnerships.

And the industry has always had to deal with periods of change. The financial challenges and layoffs associated with a number of large tech companies in late 2022 are comparable to an earlier period in 2008–09 when Yahoo, Microsoft, and AOL were declining as viable options and the industry was reeling. But of course, it was exactly at this point that Google and Facebook started to penetrate the market for digital display ads, along with a whole bunch of demand- and supply-side technology partners. That was when automated trading itself took off. And some of the most successful companies in the AdTech market—AppNexus, Magnite, MediaMath, PubMatic, The Trade Desk (TTD), to name but a few—saw birth and growth.

It is a massively challenging time. We are watching an industry grapple with defunding misinformation, hate speech, fraud, and supporting informed consent, and having its role in wider societal ills questioned (DEI, child welfare, climate change). But it's during these times that the industry tends to pivot, and change happens in both good and bad ways. Some of which advertisers themselves can influence and some they can't.

Improving transparency practices and workstreams is one of the immediate areas where they can start to do so. Part of the issue in the industry is that it has porous walls. It's hard to find the edges (we can't even agree on the scale of it).

But it's in everyone's interests to help create a more sustainable and responsible digital advertising ecosystem that protects brands, the industry, consumers, and society alike. A Jenga-style tower of ad technologies has been built, with new bits added and unwanted bits tentatively removed. As a result, we are now living with a complex system we would never consciously design with hindsight.

Some would say a lot of the critique of the digital advertising industry overrates its relative impact in comparison to the efficacy of other parts of marketing. Advertising can't be a weak force for good and a powerful force for bad simultaneously. Or can it?

It has always had societal and social currency of sorts. Everyone has a favorite ad or two, when asked. Very few though can easily name a favorite digital ad they have seen that they would like to share.

Search, social, display, and most of the other forms of digital promotion have always been at the transactional end of the funnel. Down the food chain. Bottom-of-the-funnel performance marketing. This has somewhat "juniorized" the industry. Older heavyweights and titans of agency land might be more concerned with the next creative killer intervention or the next wave of awards.

Brand controllers, and the owners of ad budgets, have approached digital the way many a grandparent would approach a PlayStation: "Let's just watch the kids do it."

Failure to adapt is the ultimate risk

Sometimes accepting the prevailing industry consensus is risky enough in itself.

"It aint what you don't know that gets you into trouble. It's what you know for sure that just aint so" (Mark Twain).

Much of the industry infrastructure has been built on the "necessity for hypertargeting." This has been the justification for most of the industry's use of (now illegal) personal identifiers, and granular profiling datasets. We have all been sold the need for "personalization" but have never had its full value demonstrated. Which is in itself now moot, given the industry privacy headwinds against it from a number of directions. The datasets on which it is founded are now illegal; they are also unreliable (even simple gender targeting was only reliable 50 percent of the time).

Beyond that, some have identified fundamental inefficiencies, leading to higher media costs. The extra fees charged by data owners for what they claim is highly targeted data are generally offset by paying less for more broadly targeted data in any case. "Broadly targeted media allows you to reach more of the right buyers at a better price point." Or as one headline put it, "Forget personalization, it's impossible and it doesn't work" (Weinberg and Lombardo, 2022).

There is also some fear associated with finding out what might be some unpalatable truths. In order to learn, we have to profess some kind of ignorance to begin with. To say you know when you know, and to say you don't when you don't, is the ultimate wisdom.

For good or bad, the new auditors and "privacy cops," as well as the "fraud police," are now necessary players in the industry. They are not here to "destroy business models" or "defund the supply chain."

They are here to help ensure that the industry doesn't implode. They are not solving privacy on the web on the one hand whilst allowing the large platforms to block measurement—that's the choice of the platforms themselves. And they are not the ones changing Twitter and scaring away content creators with verification fees—that's Twitter itself potentially doing that. Independent measurement practitioners are necessary until the industry makes their existence moot.

Skilling up your teams is critical. Those who engage in digital campaigns only by "proxy" might use the language of AdTech without necessarily understanding the workings of it. And whilst "understanding the working of something" was never a prerequisite to getting it to work for you (anyone fancy explaining broadcast media in tech terms?), the challenges the industry faces almost demand that we all get into the weeds as quickly as we can, and then get out and get practical.

As Upton Sinclair would say, "It's very difficult to get [someone] to understand something, when [their] salary depends on not understanding it" (Sinclair, 1935). And many in the space are dependent on you not.

A running mantra in agency land has always been, "give me the freedom of a dysfunctional client." Many build their reputations and careers off of the back of an advertiser who doesn't quite have their mojo, or at best doesn't have a clue.

Likewise, the sellers of AdTech solutions often depend on the rest of the industry acting complacently, akin to the "Bathing Apes" of the famous brand BAPE, which referred to the complacent overindulgence of the middle classes in Japan, and the lazy opulence of those who love to wallow in warm water. Or the snow monkeys at Jigokudani Park, who can be seen casually bathing in hot springs. Hot springs that sit on tectonic plates of disruption, if they are not careful.

It matters

The number of connected devices, processing capabilities, support technologies, and the sheer number of options open to advertisers, only grows. The only appropriate response to landscapes with continuous change is to make sure you have the resources and skillsets required to be flexible enough to respond when needed.

The internet as we know it today would not exist without the infrastructure of advertising. Juggernauts like Google and Facebook would never have had the opportunity to emerge if it wasn't for display advertising, pay-per-click, or social media-based advertising.

Every emergent media business today faces a bipolar decision—run ads or run paywalls. Now we see this playing out not only with emergent players but with established ones like Netflix and Twitter. All of the free online content and news sources that we use today exist primarily because of advertising. It's easy to draw a direct connection between clean sources of advertising inventory, quality content, and good user experiences.

The digital advertising ecosystem is changing its spots, as well as extending its reach worldwide.

As it develops and morphs, the way we develop our practices in using it will be critical.

It could be argued that digital advertising trading models have evolved around the spending of money rather than the objective of delivering success. Opaque practices siphon off far too much money between the advertiser and the desired audience, or budgets disappear down the ecosystem cracks or in mysterious trading deals. But we all work in an ecosystem that has just as many operational cracks as it does suspicious activity. In order to distinguish between the two, new skillsets and good partners are needed. The good news is that a lot of them are solvable and within reach of those advertisers who want to.

Not all advertisers necessarily put transparency at the top of their agendas. Does creative effectiveness at any cost trump transparency?

"Who wants transparency when you can have magic? Who wants prose when you can have poetry?"

Figure 8.1 Growth of internet connection worldwide

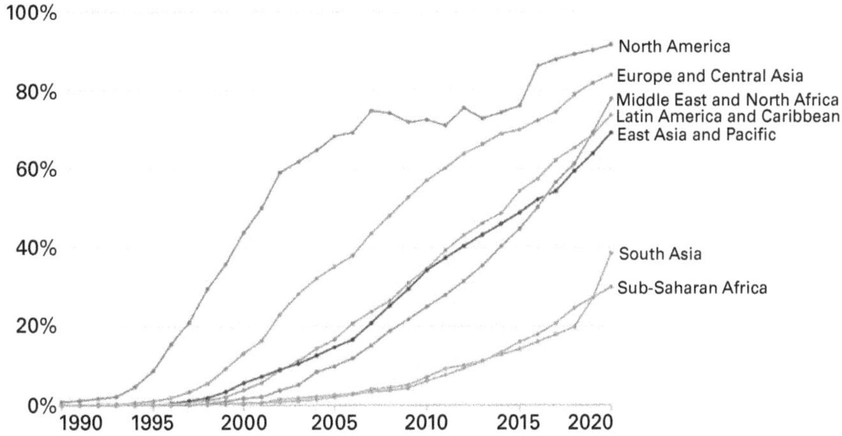

Internet usage includes computers, mobile phones, personal digital assistants, games machines, digital TVs, etc.
SOURCE Roser et al (2015)

No, not a quote from a libertarian advertiser who may reject basic governance, but from a royalist supporting the "magic" of the royal family in the TV drama *The Crown*. Sure, everyone loves a bit of drama and fantasy and escapism, but it's also at the heart of the maintenance of the worst kind of power structures. Deflection and delusion are central to good storytelling, and fine in the context of a Netflix drama, but not if you want to avoid your advertising budget falling victim to AdTech carpetbaggers. We are not meaning to directly equate the sellers of average ad technology with mediocre royal families. It's just a word of warning that some are indeed like poor magicians who can't believe they are getting away with it.

It's important to approach transparency and measurement with an even hand. You have to go into it not only knowing what you want to achieve (e.g. "where are the fraudulent sources in my buys?") but also with a clear sense of what you want to do with that info (e.g. "I want to redistribute spends, not cut them") and, critically, how ("I need to connect my raw verification data with my digital buys"). Have goals, be accurate and thorough in measurement, and make that measurement useful.

This is a plea for advertisers to embrace change. Not in the form they are used to in terms of degrees of trialing of new approaches, but in the everyday habits they foster. Ones that ensure that data and money flows can be tracked accurately. And like most change, it is best when it comes in small portions. Incremental baby steps.

It's a plea to get involved at multiple levels. With your partners, your frenemies, and wider government initiatives. Regulation needs industry collaboration. But industries move as herds—most prefer to watch patiently from the safety of the shadows until everyone moves. It's not enough just to switch off the "open market," we have to support it where we can, and hold our partners and the walled gardens to account when we can.

The industry works on your money flowing through it. To quote an anonymous buyer when asked about whether transparency efforts and tracking technologies were working: "All is looking good, money is flowing." Digital advertising has an attention deficit issue and some hidden efficiency issues that only budget holders can solve.

Global economies have been lurching from one crisis to the next over the last decade and a half. National economies are in the midst of mitigating exposures to the next recession. One of the first line items on the chopping block in corporate review is always advertising, largely as a result of it being wrongly treated as a discretionary cost rather than an investment and source of growth. Advertising budgets are perennially under pressure. And when budgets are under pressure, advertisers have traditionally rushed towards programmatic as a life saver—70 percent of advertisers in new markets enter programmatic to lower the cost of media (IAB Europe, 2018).

The two big forces driving programmatic buying in the immediate future will be (1) those who are economically challenged and need immediate returns, and (2) those who will look for efficiency gains from an inefficient supply chain.

Ultimately this involves things that are dependent on good feedback loops—strategies and tactics. Effectiveness and efficiencies. Things that have always obsessed the good and bad folks in adland.

Approaching any of these problems will demand direct addressing of the quality issues that plague the digital ecosystem. And forming necessary partnerships because you can't do it all— with agency groups, on the one hand, held accountable for outcomes, and advertisers themselves leaning into technology partnerships in key areas e.g. working with a supply chain technology vendor.

What is important on the internet is the quality of traffic. There is an existing and growing market inefficiency in digital advertising, at the scale of billions of dollars. As things stand, quality assurance at the individual advertiser level is the only productive way for the industry to move forward.

An open, safe, advertiser-funded digital ecosystem. The notion that everything on the web should be free is a false one. The internet needs to be supported financially. Great content costs money. There are a lot of human labor costs and technology costs. We need to ensure that advertisers are comfortable investing in it as it stands. It's not enough just to switch off the open market from your planning. We are living with the unintended consequences of a complex system that we, as an industry, would never proactively design in the first place.

We need to fix it or lose it. Or we will be left with an advertising industry that is conflicted, and media strategies that are struggling for direction. Tensions will include those that exist between people's rights and the expectations around privacy and the technology we use. Clear, enforceable, and enforced laws on privacy will help. There are currently too many gray zones across markets on what does and does not constitute personal information in terms of the by-products of the bidding system. And quite a few unknowns as to how the large tech platforms' landscape will develop.

But advertising should lean in where and how it can. Deploying measurement in a privacy-friendly manner, unobstructed, changes its own paradigm. The goal should not necessarily be simply to isolate wastage and reduce spend, it should be to make sure that your money goes to places where it was intended and that it serves a purpose for your business.

No pressure.

References

BARB (2022) BARB makes Netflix viewing reporting widely available, https://www.barb.co.uk/news/barb-makes-netflix-viewing-reporting-widely-available/ (archived at https://perma.cc/G8L8-HSXM)

Boyle, A (2022) The chaos of privacy compliance in the US, *Ad Exchanger*, https://www.adexchanger.com/privacy/the-chaos-of-privacy-compliance-in-the-us/ (archived at https://perma.cc/68BA-RPVY)

Dentsu (2022) 2023 Media Trends, https://www.dentsu.com/hu/en/our-latest-thinking/media-trends-2023 (archived at https://perma.cc/YT6R-N2K4)

EU Commission (2020) EU Commission Antitrust Statement of Objections, https://ec.europa.eu/commission/presscorner/detail/en/ip_22_7728 (archived at https://perma.cc/VUF9-4QFW)

Hanoch, Y (2021) The robot made me do it: Human–robot interaction and risk-taking behavior, *Cyberpsychology, Behavior, and Social Networking*, **24** (5), pp 337–42

IAB Europe (2018) IAB Europe Report: Attitudes to programmatic advertising 2018, https://iabeurope.eu/research-thought-leadership/iab-europe-report-attitudes-to-programmatic-advertising-2018/ (archived at https://perma.cc/J67R-8JA4)

IPA (2014) Prof. Daniel Kahneman talks Behavioral Economics with Rory Sutherland at the Institute of Practitioners of Advertising, London, *YouTube*, https://www.youtube.com/watch?v=ggrwrpq3VAk (archived at https://perma. cc/9ENQ-9ZTL)

ISBA, PWC and AOP (2020) Programmatic Supply Chain Transparency Study, https://www.isba.org.uk/media/2424/executive-summary-programmatic-supply-chain-transparency-study.pdf (archived at https://perma.cc/9P8D-9H9G)

Joseph, S (2022) Global economic crisis sparks reappraisal of online ad spending by brand marketers, *DigiDay*, https://digiday.com/marketing/global-economic-crisis-sparks-reappraisal-of-online-ad-spending-by-brand-marketers/ (archived at https://perma.cc/YY47-KYB8)

Roser, M, Ritchie, H and Ortiz-Ospina, E (2015) Internet, *Our World in Data*, https://ourworldindata.org/internet (archived at https://perma.cc/7C6U-RQVM)

Shields, R (2022) Apple is building a demand-side platform, *DigiDay*, https://digiday.com/media/apple-is-building-a-demand-side-platform/ (archived at https://perma.cc/AUX3-ED8Q)

Sinclair, U (1935) *I, Candidate for Governor*, Farrar & Reinhart Inc

WARC (2022) The Marketer's Toolkit For 2023, https://www.warc.com/reports/toolkit (archived at https://perma.cc/FZ5F-66YX)

Waters (2022) Nick Waters 'Harder to dispute': Why advertisers are slowing spending in the Google-Facebook duopoly, *eBiquity*, https://www.ebiquity.com/news-insights/press/harder-to-dispute-why-advertisers-are-slowing-spending-in-the-google-facebook-duopoly/ (archived at https://perma.cc/XS5W-JEPP)

Weinberg, P and Lombardo, J (2022) Forget personalization, it's impossible and it doesn't work, *Marketing Week*, https://www.marketingweek.com/peter-weinberg-jon-lombardo-personalisation-impersonalisation/ (archived at https://perma.cc/A9YL-P3ME)

WFA (2022) Marketing budgets under heavy scrutiny, WFA and Ebiquity research, https://wfanet.org/knowledge/item/2022/10/13/Marketing-budgets-under-heavy-scrutiny-WFA-and-Ebiquity-research (archived at https://perma.cc/C4RS-VNDY)

Wiener, L et al (2022) How retail media is reshaping retail, *Boston Consulting Group*, https://www.bcg.com/en-ca/publications/2022/how-media-is-shaping-retail (archived at https://perma.cc/AAF6-SUNJ)

GLOSSARY

AANA Australian Association of National Advertisers. An Australian trade association representing advertisers' interests.

ad exchange The central computerized marketplace that connects the buy side and sell side.

ad network A bundler of ad opportunities from different publishers, offering the bundles for sale.

ad server A machine that stores an ad, delivers it to your laptop or phone, and captures some metrics as a result.

ad verification A technology service that allows advertisers to check whether their ads are seen by real people, in the right geography, and in safe and suitable environments.

Ads.txt Like a public record of authorized sellers of ad opportunities. Comes in the form of a text file that contains "authorized digital sellers" and where a publisher records who can sell inventory on the site.

adserver logs Granular data that is collected about every single ad delivered (from the ad server).

AI Artificial Intelligence. Automated decision making that approximates that of a human. It's here, and about to make and eat our lunches.

ANA Association of National Advertisers. A US trade association representing advertisers' interests.

ATT App Tracking Transparency. The restriction that Apple now imposes to get access to apple device identifiers (see IDFA); it requires websites and apps to obtain explicit permission from users before being granted access to IDFA.

AVBs Agency Volume Bonuses. Revenue, or the value equivalent, that agencies can get from some media owners or publishers, that may or may not be declared to an advertiser.

AWS Amazon Web Services. The part of Amazon that provides cloud computing, data processing, storage, and analytics services.

BAME Black, Asian and Minority Ethnic. A phrase used in the UK for diversity measurements. Somewhat outdated.

bid ID Data label or identifier (in the DSP log) used to describe the specific trading bid.

bid request This happens when a user visits a website with ad opportunities on it. This request (containing descriptors about the ad opportunity) goes from the publisher's website to the ad exchange, which passes it on to the buy-side systems for them to make "bid" or "no bid" decisions. All done in the blink of an eye.

bid stream The stream of data that comes from publishers and apps on the sell side that contains basic facts about the ad opportunity on offer to the buy side.

Big Tech Commonly used to refer to the large dominant players such as Google, Facebook, Amazon, Apple, etc. Often used in adland in a derogatory manner akin to "Big Pharma" or "Big Tobacco" in other industries.

brand safety and suitability Brand safety, in the strictest sense, refers to environments where brands can advertise safely without being adjacent to a pre-defined list of negative content or environments. Brand suitability refers to where specific brands can find their specific relevance in positive and brand-appropriate environments.

CCPA California Consumer Privacy Act. A state-wide consumer privacy law comparable, but slightly different, to GDPR in the EU (see GDPR).

CDP Customer Data Platform. A system for managing data used by agencies, advertisers, or publishers, which tends to use first-party data. Not to be confused with a DMP, which uses third-party data.

Closed Web In the context of advertising, used to describe the (data) restricted "Walled Gardens" such as Facebook, etc.

cookie A small piece of code, saved on a user's browser, that enables the tracking of user behavior during a website visit. First-party cookies are owned by the website owner. Third-party cookies are owned by someone else and not native to the website in question.

count on download vs bids won (counts) Two different ways to count impressions (see Impressions). One based on impressions "won" at bidding (see "Bid stream"), the other based on counts of ads actually served downloaded to a user's browser or device.

CPG Consumer Packaged Goods. A type of advertiser (sometimes referred to as **FMCG** Fast-Moving Consumer Goods).

CPM Cost Per Mille. The cost for 1,000 impressions (see Impressions).

CTV Connected Television, or TV devices that are connected to the web and that can stream video content or hold apps that do so (not to be confused with the more generic "OTT").

Dark Web The part of the web that is only accessible via the use of specific types of software, or with limited or restricted access. Not a nice neighborhood.

data segments Audience segments, usually predefined and packaged up for selling to advertisers by third-party technology and data partners.

DAU Daily Active Users. A quantification of the number of active users of a platform.

DEI Diversity, Equity, and Inclusion. A policy promoting the full, fair, and equitable participation of all in the workplace.

demand side Brands and agencies on the "buy" side of the digital ad trading marketplace. Some think it is only the brand advertiser that is truly on the demand side.

deterministic vs. probabilistic (measurement) A deterministic measure is one where the data speaks for itself and the indicators are clear. Counting the data is enough. A probabilistic measure is one where the answer is dependent on some assumptions or modeling. Doing some mathematical somersaults with the data, and not just counting it, is required.

direct bookings The manual (not automated) booking of digital ads, usually for a fixed price.

DLT Distributed Ledger Technology. A shared database of information with an agreed truth, shared and duplicated across multiple devices or storage locations. Like a flexible but unchangeable record of e.g. transactions that some promise could revolutionize ad trading.

DMP Data Management Platform. A system for managing data used by agencies, advertisers, or publishers, which tends to use third-party data. Not to be confused with a CDP, which uses first-party data.

DSP Demand-Side Platform. A software tool or platform that allows brands and agencies on the buy side to bid on available ad opportunities. Linked to supply-side platforms via ad exchanges. Logs granular data that is collected about every single ad traded (from the DSP).

dynamic creative optimization (DCO) Refers to (a promised approach of) delivering the right message at the right time in order to maximize the likelihood of advertising impact. It's a process where nuanced variations of a particular creative are served in an efficient manner based on incoming signals relating to, e.g. different types of audiences, in different contexts.

exchange ID Data label or identifier (in the DSP log) used to describe the ad exchange used in the trade.

exoneration vs incrimination (fraud detection) Exoneration techniques in fraud detection assume everything is a bot until "signs of a human" are detected. Incrimination techniques assume everything is human unless "signs of bots" are detected.

first-party data Data obtained from brand-owned sources or media owner web pages. It's extremely valuable if handled with care, but toxic if not.

frequency capping A technique that is supposed to limit the number of times each of us is exposed to the same ad. This is clearly not working.

FTE Full-Time Equivalent. A method used to quantify, for example, how many hours of a full-time employee are being sold by an agency to an advertiser.

GCP Google Cloud Platform. The part of Google that offers cloud computing services, data processing, storage, and analytics.

GDPR The General Data Protection Regulation. An EU legislative beast that, in 2018, set in stone the requirements around the protection of consumer privacies. And gave birth to millions of lawyers.

GPU Graphics Processing Unit. An essential part of the image processing capability of devices like computers and smartphones. The basis of some deterministic fraud detection techniques (see Deterministic vs. Probabilistic fraud detection techniques).

ID graph A unified view of e.g. a user or device based on their interactions and behaviors across the web. The basis of the promises around ad personalization (see Personalization).

ID Identifiers Pieces of data that enable the identification of a person, a device.

IDFA Identifier For Advertisers. Sometimes referred to as the Apple ID. A unique random device identifier Apple generates and assigns to every device. In 2020, Apple announced plans to restrict access to IDFA and require websites and apps to obtain explicit permission from users (see ATT).

impression Made in reference to when an ad creative is fetched and shown to a user. It's countable, the backbone of ad trading, and you might think it's straightforward, but as you will see in the book, it's not.

impression ID Data label or identifier (in the ad server log) used to describe the specific ad impression generated.

In-Geo The part of ad verification (see Ad Verification) that allows advertisers to check whether their ads are seen in the right geography.

IoT Internet Of Things. A promised future where a multitude of physical things have processing capacity, are smart, and connected.

IP address A unique identifier for each device using the web (Internet Protocol) to communicate over a network.

ISBA Incorporated Society of British Advertisers. A UK trade association representing advertisers' interests.

IVT Invalid Traffic. Any impression counts, or activity, that don't come from a real user. Can be the result of bots, or other nefarious activity.

log-level data granular data that is collected about every single ad traded (from the DSP) or ad delivered (from the Ad Server).

MAU Monthly Active Users. A quantification of the number of active users of a platform.

metaverse A promised future which is some kind of persistent bridge between the physical and digital worlds with interactivity. Currently boiled down to gaming or collaborating with headsets.

ML Machine Learning. How a machine develops its intelligence through training against a provided dataset, and using a multitude of techniques. Not to be confused with AI, which is the output of good ML. "Good ML gives birth to AI."

MMP Mobile Measurement Partner. A company that helps measure campaign performance across mobile advertising marketing channels, media sources, and ad networks.

MRC Media Rating Council. A US-based entity that manages the industry accreditation for measurement services like ratings provision and ad verification. Like credit ratings agencies in the financial markets, but for marketing measurement.

MSA Master Service Agreement. The type of agreement that governs the relationship between many advertisers and agencies.

Open Web In the context of advertising, used to describe the sources of ad opportunities (and data) that are available outside of the restricted "Walled Gardens" such as Facebook etc.

OTS Opportunity to See. The number of opportunities a particular individual, or group, has to see a served ad.

OTT "Over The Top" delivery of content. A means of delivery of content that bypasses traditional broadcast or cable, consumed on many types of devices (not to be confused with the more specific CTV).

personalization A phrase used by those in the digital ad industry when trying to describe the use of data for refined targeting purposes. In theory, we should all be seeing ads that are extremely relevant to who we are and what we want. Which clearly is not yet the case.

placement ID Data label or identifier (in the ad server log) used to describe the specific location where an ad will be shown.

PMP Private Marketplace. A private advertising auction. It's still a real-time bidding environment but it's not a public one—advertisers can only access the private marketplace with an invitation.

post-bid Measurement that provides insight after bidding takes place. Usually in the context of verification methods.

pre-bid Data or analysis that facilitates decision making before any bid takes place. Can refer to targeting or verification methods.

programmatic The buying of digital advertising space done automatically via the use of technology partners and data sources.

robots.txt A standard used by websites to try to control bad behaviour of bot "crawlers." A way for a website to try and corral to control visiting bots.

RTB Real-Time Bidding. The use of auctions through which ad opportunities are bought and sold. Done on an automated, real-time basis. Hence the name.

sellers.json A publicly available file of information pertaining to the sellers of any ad opportunities, where publishers can elect to share their individual name or business name with the buy side.

SEO Search Engine Optimization. The process of using available tools to maximize the visibility of a brand or a website when people are searching for products or services.

server side vs. client side (environment) Used to describe where a bit of code actually runs. The "client" in this context is how an engineer refers to the end user's device. "Client side" refers to everything in a web application that is displayed or takes place on this end user's device. "Server side" means everything that happens on the server, instead of on the client, away from the end user. Think your living room with your shiny new MacBook, versus a cavernous underground data center with thousands of servers.

SLA Service-Level Agreement. The part of a contract that helps guarantee the service level being provided by a supplier to an advertiser.

source URL Data label or identifier (in the DSP log) used to describe the specific web address (URL) in question.

SOW Scope of Work. The part of a contract between an advertiser and any service supplier that outlines the scope of services being provided.

SPO Supply Path Optimization. A process through which advertisers and their buyers can efficiently streamline their access to quality sources of advertising opportunities.

SSAI Server-Side Ad Insertion. Not as painful as it sounds. It's the process where an ad is embedded as part of the piece of main content being consumed. Not the way that traditional web ads on your laptops run (which is based on client-side ad insertion, see server-side vs. client side).

SSP Supply-Side Platform. A software tool or platform that allows publishers on the sell side to sell available ad opportunities. Linked to demand-side platforms via ad exchanges.

STEM Science, Technology, Engineering, and Math.

supply-side Publishers, apps, and audience sources on the "sell" side of the digital ad trading marketplace. Some think everyone other than the brand is on the supply side.

TCF Transparency and Consent Framework. The industry's attempt to make the digital trading ecosystem align with the emergent legal requirements around user privacy protection.

tech stack The set of data and tech partners that an advertiser or agency needs to engage in digital planning and buying.

tech tax A phrase that is used to describe the difference between what an advertiser pays, and what a publisher gets, minus the ad agency fees. Basically a gripe about all of the other monies that go to all of the intermediaries (and necessary technologies) involved in digital advertising.

third-party data Data obtained from sources other than your own, and stitched together to provide "target groups" for advertising. Openly bought and sold in the marketplace. Its demise always seems imminent.

trading desk A team that is tasked with buying digital ads and using demand-side tools to do so. They can sit in an agency, within an agency-third party, or within a brand advertiser. What they do is often more important than where they do it.

viewability A metric that measures the degree to which an ad is viewed. A standardized, if somewhat arbitrary, industry definition of what can be considered to be "in view" and hence count as a viewed impression (as opposed to simply an impression based on an ad served).

WFA World Federation of Advertisers. A global trade association representing advertisers' interests.

ABOUT THE AUTHORS

Shailin Dhar is based in New York City and is the founding partner of Method Media Intelligence (MMI). He is a media, web technology, and ad technology expert who is focused on helping companies confirm digital ad efficacy, secure validity, evaluate viewability, and support brand safety. After working in the other side of the industry, he now works with brands, agencies, global trade groups, ad-tech firms, and ad verification companies to reduce fraudulent and opaque business practices in the digital advertising market, and readying marketers for future challenges.

Scott Thomson is based in London and is a partner in Method Media Intelligence (MMI), a measurement consultancy and technology provider. After working with a Ministry of Defence contractor helping design user-friendly control systems, he has spent 25 years with companies like Publicis, Nielsen, Media Audits, Naked Communications, and Dentsu, focusing on helping brands devise, design, and measure successful marketing strategies, and working with numerous global brands across multiple geographies on many of the challenges currently faced by the advertising industry.

INDEX

CPSIA information can be obtained
at www.ICGtesting.com
Printed in the USA
JSHW070145250423
40763JS00008B/11

9 781398 609662